Creative Stitches

for Contemporary Embroidery

Visual Guide to 120 Essential Stitches
for Stunning Designs

Sharon Boggon

C&T PUBLISHING

Text, photography, and copyright © 2020 by Sharon Boggon

Publisher: Amy Barrett-Daffin

Creative Director: Gailen Runge

Acquisitions Editor: Roxane Cerda

Managing Editor: Liz Aneloski

Editor: Karla Menaugh

Technical Editor: Debbie Rodgers

Cover/Book Designer: April Mostek

Production Coordinator: Zinnia Heinzmann

Production Editor: Alice Mace Nakanishi

Photography by Sharon Boggon and Jerry Everard

Library of Congress Cataloging-in-Publication Data

Names: Boggon, Sharon, 1956- author.

Title: Creative stitches for contemporary embroidery : visual guide to 120 essential stitches for stunning designs / Sharon Boggon.

Description: Lafayette, CA : C&T Publishing, [2020] | Includes index.

Identifiers: LCCN 2020019612 | ISBN 9781617458774 (paperback) | ISBN 9781617458781 (ebook)

Subjects: LCSH: Embroidery. | Stitches (Sewing)

Classification: LCC TT770 .B64 2020 | DDC 746.44--dc23

LC record available at https://lccn.loc.gov/2020019612

Printed in the USA

10 9 8 7 6 5 4 3 2

◇ Summer Beach Days contemporary embroidery panel

Dedication

For my husband, Jerry, and my daughter, Eve

Acknowledgments

I would like to thank my ever-patient husband, Jerry Everard, for his work producing the photography in this book and his unfailing belief in what I do. Also, thanks go to my daughter, Eve Everard, for putting up with my creative passion for all things fabric and stitch.

In my stitching life, I have been influenced by numerous people. I have been fortunate to have stitching friends both online and offline who have supported me and taught me much. Thanks go out to the stitching community that willingly shares.

Contents

§ Fabric postcard using French knots (page 135), bullion knots (page 41), and cast-on stitch (page 78) worked on linen, perle cotton, wool,
§ embroidery floss, and linen thread

THE STITCHES

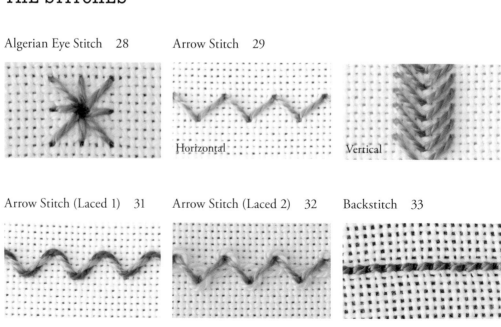

Horizontal

Vertical

Backstitch (Beaded) 34

Backstitch (Threaded) 35

Backstitch (Threaded Stacked) 36

Backstitch (Trellis Stitch) 38

Backstitch (Whipped) 39

Basque Stitch 40

Bullion Knot 41

Buttonhole Stitch (*also* Blanket Stitch) 43

Buttonhole Stitch (Alternating) 45

Buttonhole Stitch (Alternating Up-and-Down) 47

Buttonhole Stitch (Bar) 49

Buttonhole Stitch (*var.* Barb Stitch) 51

Buttonhole Stitch (*var.* Battlement Stitch) 52

Buttonhole Stitch (Beaded) 54

Buttonhole Stitch (Closed) 55

Buttonhole Stitch (Crossed) 56

Buttonhole Stitch (Double) 57

Buttonhole Stitch (Fringed) 58

Buttonhole Stitch (Herring) 60

Buttonhole Stitch (Interlaced Up-and-Down) 62

Buttonhole Stitch (Knotted) 63

Buttonhole Stitch (Reversed Bar) 64

Buttonhole Stitch (Threaded Alternating) 65

Buttonhole Stitch (Triangular) 66

Buttonhole Stitch
(Up-and-Down) 67

Buttonhole Stitch
(Wheel) 68

Buttonhole Stitch
(Wheel Cup) 70

Buttonhole Stitch
(Whipped) 72

Buttonhole Stitch
(Whipped Alternating) 73

Buttonhole Stitch
(Zigzag Up-and-Down) 74

Cable Chain Stitch 75

Cable Chain Stitch
(Buttonholed) 76

Cable Chain Stitch
(Knotted) 77

Cast-On Stitch 78

Chain Stitch 80

Chain Stitch
(*var.* Berry Stitch) 81

Chain Stitch (Butterfly) 82

Chain Stitch
(Chained Bar) 83

Chain Stitch (Detached)
(*also* Lazy Daisy Stitch) 84

Chain Stitch (Feathered) 85

Chain Stitch
(Long-Tail) 86

Chain Stitch
(*var.* Oyster Stitch) 87

Chain Stitch (Threaded) 88

Chain Stitch (Triple) 89

Chain Stitch
(*var.* Tulip Stitch) 91

Chain Stitch (Twisted) 93

Chain Stitch
(Whipped 1) 94

Chain Stitch
(Whipped 2) 95

Chain Stitch
(Whipped Long-Tail)   96

Chain Stitch
(Whipped Triple)   97

Chain Stitch
(Woven Detached)   98

Chain Stitch (Zigzag)   99

Chevron Stitch   100

Chevron Stitch
(Double)   101

Chevron Stitch
(Fringed)   102

Chevron Stitch
(Half-Chevron)   103

Chevron Stitch
(Herringbone)   105

Chevron Stitch
(Squared)   106

Chevron Stitch
(Stepped)   108

Coral Stitch   109

Couching   110

Cretan Stitch   111

Cretan Stitch
(Herringbone)   114

Cretan Stitch (Looped)   115

Cross-Stitch   117

Cross-Stitch (Raised)   118

Cross-Stitch (Woven)   119

Drizzle Stitch   120

Drizzle Stitch (Double)   122

Feather Stitch   124

Feather Stitch
(and Chain)   125

Feather Stitch
(Knotted)   126

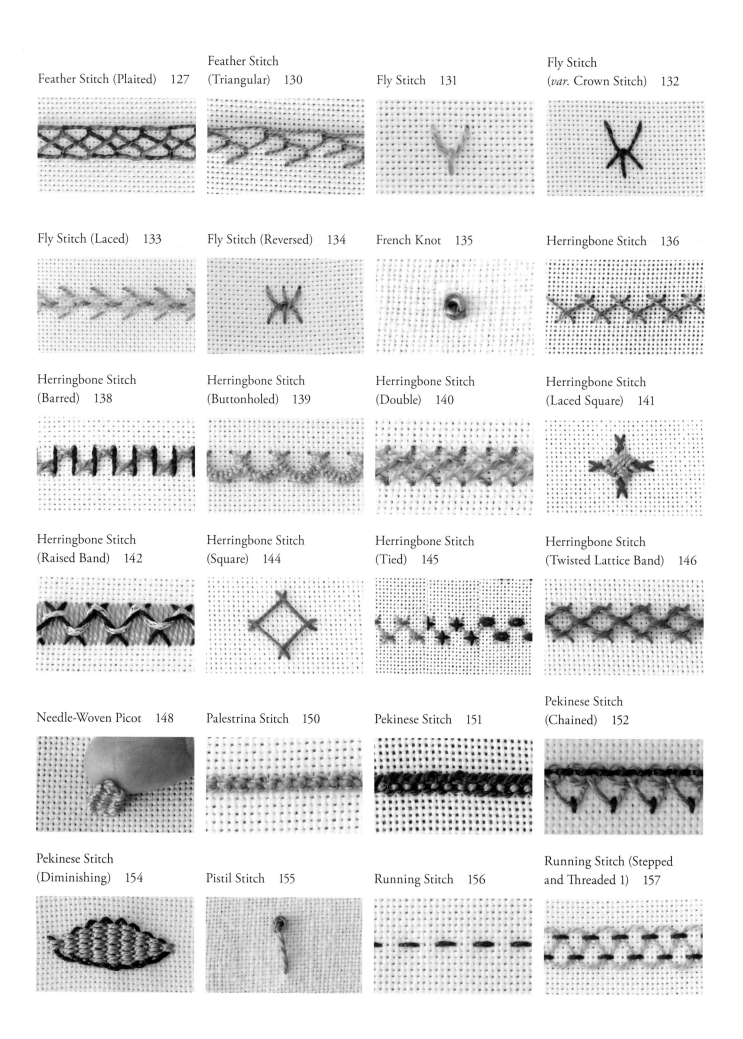

Feather Stitch (Plaited)   127

Feather Stitch (Triangular)   130

Fly Stitch   131

Fly Stitch (*var.* Crown Stitch)   132

Fly Stitch (Laced)   133

Fly Stitch (Reversed)   134

French Knot   135

Herringbone Stitch   136

Herringbone Stitch (Barred)   138

Herringbone Stitch (Buttonholed)   139

Herringbone Stitch (Double)   140

Herringbone Stitch (Laced Square)   141

Herringbone Stitch (Raised Band)   142

Herringbone Stitch (Square)   144

Herringbone Stitch (Tied)   145

Herringbone Stitch (Twisted Lattice Band)   146

Needle-Woven Picot   148

Palestrina Stitch   150

Pekinese Stitch   151

Pekinese Stitch (Chained)   152

Pekinese Stitch (Diminishing)   154

Pistil Stitch   155

Running Stitch   156

Running Stitch (Stepped and Threaded 1)   157

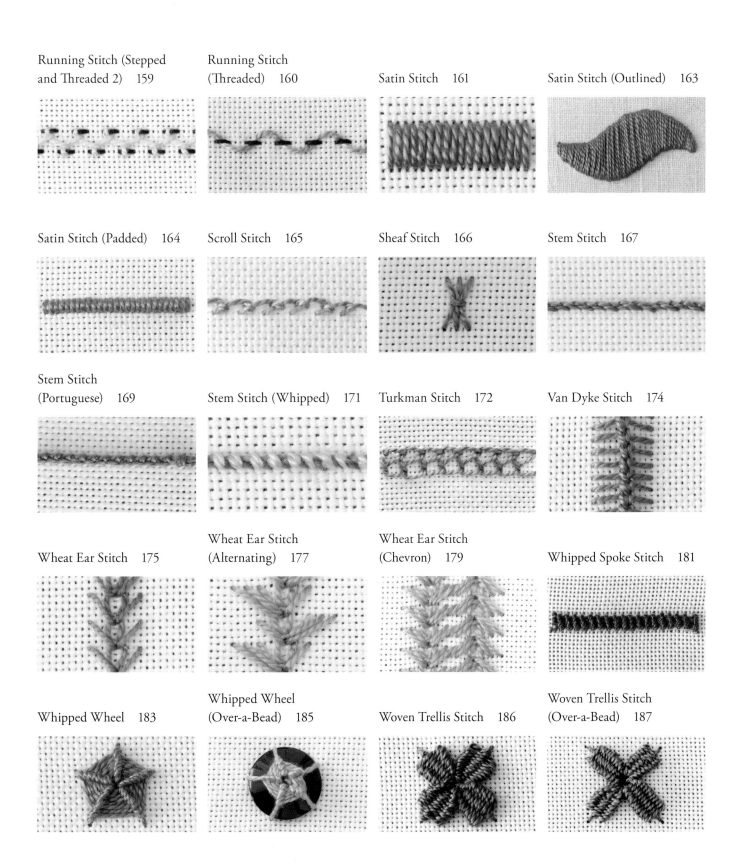

Introduction

With this book, I invite you to join me on a creative path via creative embroidery. I aim to introduce you to a way of thinking about hand stitching that not only teaches you to embroider, but also gives you the tools to improvise and adapt stitches to your needs.

Contemporary hand embroidery is a form of self-expression. As you stitch, you will make dozens of small choices, such as choosing a fabric, a stitch, a thread, a color, the thickness of thread, size and spacing of stitches, and so on. Through these small, personal decisions, you express yourself.

As you stitch, resist comparing your creative work with others, and don't worry about being perfect. Exploring your creative self is not a competition. How can you compete with something that can't be measured? Competition undermines creativity.

Perfectionism freezes all creativity. As humans we are not perfect. Of course, we strive to improve and be better at what we do, but there is a great difference between aiming to improve, and perfection.

Handmade items are a little bit wobbly, a little uneven, and you relate to them because they leave a trace of the hand that made them. They are human rather than perfect.

There is very little right or wrong in contemporary textile practice, just methods of working that are suitable for what you are making, and other methods that are unsuitable.

What do I mean by methods that are suitable and unsuitable? To give you an example, if you make a garment, obviously it has to be stitched so that it will hold together. This will influence the process. If the garment is to be embellished with embroidery, this will also influence your choice of stitches. The stitching will need to be washable and reasonably hard-wearing. That constraint will influence your creative choices.

On the other hand, if you are making something for purely decorative purposes, the item may need to hang on a wall, or it may be small—such as a fabric postcard. Because these items are to be used in different ways, their use will influence the type of embellishment you might choose.

Remember these few ideas as you stitch, because these ideas can be liberating, particularly if you have ever had a needlework teacher negatively criticize your efforts. Enjoy your journey and sit and relax with your stitching, as the embroidery police have long gone. It's time to banish them from your head too!

◇ Detail from a fabric book page

Tools and Supplies

Supplies

Fabrics

You can use just about any fabric for contemporary creative embroidery. Of course, some fabrics are better than others. For instance, a stretchy fabric is not ideal fabric for hand embroidery. It can be done, by interfacing the back of the fabric, but it is not ideal. Some of the fabrics you can use easily are linen, cotton (including quilting cotton), silk, rayon, wool, linen/cotton blends, or wool/silk blends.

Also, look for the many specialty fabrics that are even-weave. An even-weave fabric is a cloth woven with the same number of threads per inch in both directions, so the weave creates a regular, square grid. This means you can easily stitch on a grid—instead of marking, just follow the weave of the threads to work a straight line.

§ Selection of hand
§ embroidery threads

§ Even-weave specialty
§ embroidery fabrics

Threads

Using a variety of threads can lift your stitching from the mundane to an interesting textural feast. The trick is to use a range of threads to experiment and see what is possible. Try to develop a thread stash that includes different fibers of varying thickness and textures.

Exploring creative embroidery is your excuse to experiment with the huge variety of threads available! Cotton, perle cotton, silk, rayon, metallic, chenille, silk ribbon, and ribbon floss are just a few threads that you can use with creative surface stitchery.

Most people start by using stranded cotton or embroidery floss, as that is what they have to hand and it comes in many colors. Embroidery floss has six strands that you can divide. The thread has a good drape, so you can easily twist it around your needle. For very fine-detailed stitching, you can use one or two strands. For embroidery that is more dramatic, you need to use the full six strands of your stranded cotton.

Perle cotton is a nondivisible thread used for many styles of surface embroidery. I suggest you experiment with #5, #8, and #12, as perle cotton has a tight twist which means it stitches up with a firmer texture compared to stranded cotton floss. This means your stitches will sit slightly higher when worked in perle cotton.

Silk, wool, rayon, ribbon, metallic, and novelty yarns also are used in hand-embroidery threads.

- **Silk** has a life and a built in "wow" factor, but it is expensive.

- **Wool** covers an area quickly. It fills out easily and yet is soft.

- **Rayon** has a high shine but tangles easily.

- **Metallic threads** add glitz to your embroidery.

- **Fine ribbon** can be used for embroidery. Ribbons for stitching are available in varying widths, from a narrow ⅛″ to ½″.

- **Novelty threads** can be fuzzy, bobbly, hairy, metallic, or textured in one way or another. These are usually couched (page 110) to the fabric and mostly act as a feature thread. Used with discernment, they can add real life to a project. The trick is to experiment, and mix together different fibers, thicknesses, and colors.

Once you start buying threads, you will find that keeping them in control is the challenge! I wind most of my threads onto bobbins and sort them by color. I do this because, when I am looking for a thread, I am usually looking for an interesting color contrast. For example, I might be looking for an apricot to act as a foil against a blue. I don't think to myself that I need a cotton thread or wool thread; I reach for color. So I store my threads by color.

◇ Selection of hand-dyed embroidery threads

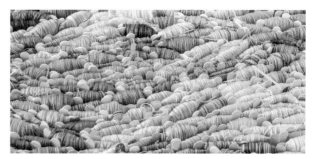

◇ A variety of embroidery threads grouped by color

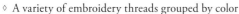

Tools and Other Equipment

Needles

Choose your fabric first, your thread second, and your needle last. Look for a needle where the thread can go through the eye with a reasonable amount of ease, while ensuring the eye is not so large as to cause the thread to rub and fray as you stitch. Check to see if the needle slides through the fabric easily, as a fabric with a tight weave will need a different needle from a fabric with a loose weave.

◇ Selection of needles

When using a variety of threads, you will need to use a variety of needles. Keep a selection of embroidery needles, tapestry needles, and milliners needles on hand. All of these can be purchased in packets of mixed sizes.

• Use milliners or straw needles when working knotted stitches. Most embroidery needles have an eye that is wider than the shaft of the needle, which means that any stitch, such as bullion knot (page 41), that wraps the thread around the needle often risks getting too tight to pull the thread through. Milliners or straw needles have an eye the same width as the diameter of the shaft, which makes sliding the wrapped bullion knot along the needle easy. These needles work for any stitch where part of the process involves wrapping the thread around the needle and then taking the needle through those wraps to complete the stitch.

• For laced and threaded stitches, use a blunt-ended tapestry needle to weave a second thread through the foundation stitches. The blunt end of the needle helps you avoid splitting the foundation row during the lacing.

• If you like adding beads to your work, add a packet of beading needles and a tapestry #26 needle to your shopping list.

Hoops and Stretchers

Stitch with a hoop or a stretcher to keep the project under an even tension. There are many stretchers, frames, and hoops on the market, but I find I reach for a hoop on most projects.

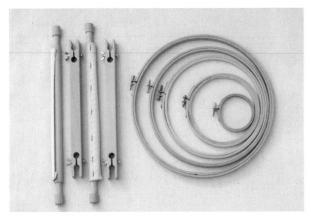

◇ Selection of hoops and stretcher bars

Markers and Quilters Pencils

You will find there are times when you need to mark your stitching lines on your fabric. Invest in some pencils and markers that are available for quilters. These pens are designed to disappear, either with a mist of water (water-erasable), or over time (air-erasable). What works on one type of fabric will not work on another, so I have a selection of pens and pencils. These can be found in stores that specialize in needlework and quilting.

◇ Selection of pencils and markers designed for quilters

A Doodle Cloth

Keep a scrap of fabric on hand where you can try out the stitches. When learning a stitch, break the learning process into two steps.

Start with a free-form sample on a small piece of fabric. This is often called a doodle cloth; it is any scrap fabric you have to hand. At this stage, don't worry about making every single stitch the same size, the same spacing, or even keeping it on the line. Just focus on the rhythm of the stitch. Give yourself a chance to get in the swing of things with the correct hand movements.

Once you have learned the stitch, aim to be more controlled. This is where you master keeping the stitch the same size, on the line, and generally looking a bit tidier.

Why work this way? If you start off with a free-form sample, you can learn the hand motion and rhythm of the stitch before trying to bring it into control. It can be difficult if you try to master two skill areas at once. So, break the learning process into two parts, work free-form first, then control. One step at a time is a walk, two steps is a jump. Walk first!

Notebook

Keep a notebook or visual journal next to you as you stitch and note stitch combinations that you think of while sewing. Also, keep it beside you when you are online and take notes of anything you see. This not only helps you remember ideas, but also develops a practice of paying attention to your own good ideas!

Give Your Stitches a Modern Twist

Embroiderers through the ages have improvised, adapted, and reinvented stitches. Much of the skill in contemporary embroidery is knowing how to give traditional stitches a new life. You will find that It is exciting to discover new uses and contexts for traditional stitches, while stretching your creative skills.

Find the Play Points

There are many ways to adapt and improvise while stitching. When you learn a stitch, look at how the stitch is structured and what shape it forms. Pay attention to what hand movements you perform as you make the stitch. Break down the structure and hand movements into parts and notice which particular action creates which part of the stitch.

As you stitch, watch for the shape formed by a single stitch as compared with the shape formed by groups or units of stitches. The more you stitch, the more you will notice that you can repeat these shapes by arranging the units in different ways. These are "play points"—points in the process where a creative decision turns a mundane stitch into a lively and interesting surface.

The more stitches you learn, the more you will see that stitches are made up of components. These also are moments in the process that allow for creative play. As you become familiar with the stitches, you will notice at some point, that this stitch and that stitch have a similar structure or a similar hand movement. Then, one day it will pop into your mind to substitute one component of a stitch with another component of a different stitch. In other words, you start to play creatively with the stitches. That is a day to celebrate, as you have started to invent with your needle and create your own stitching vocabulary.

◊ Small panel of highly textured and voided embroidery work

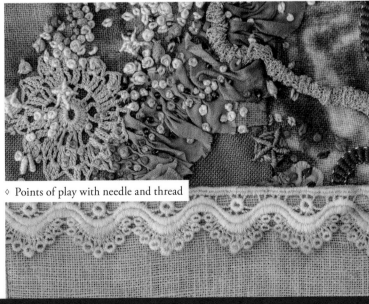

◊ Points of play with needle and thread

Creating Interesting Lines

Linear stitches are stitches such as backstitch (page 33), chain stitch (page 80), stem stitch (page 167), and running stitch (page 156) that are most often worked in a single line. Stitchers use linear stitches in designs that consist of line work, or to outline shapes.

You can vary the line created by these stitches by weaving a second thread through them—as in threaded chain stitch (page 88). Another way to change linear stitches is to whip them so that they stand slightly proud of the surface. See whipped chain (page 94), whipped stem (page 171) and whipped backstitch (page 39).

Whenever you use a second thread in a stitch, this is a play point, as you can vary the thread color, thread thickness, or texture. These stitches can be further enhanced by combining them with textured threads that can be couched (page 110) to the surface of the fabric. Other linear stitches, such as Portuguese stem stitch (page 169), scroll stitch (page 165), and Palestrina stitch (page 150) create interesting textured lines.

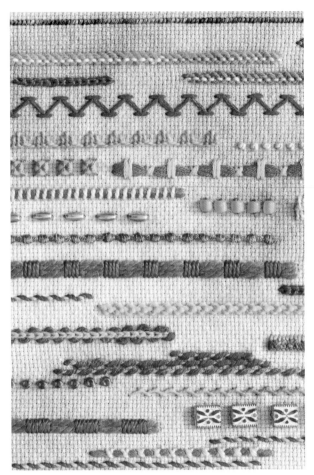

◇ Sampler of linear stitches

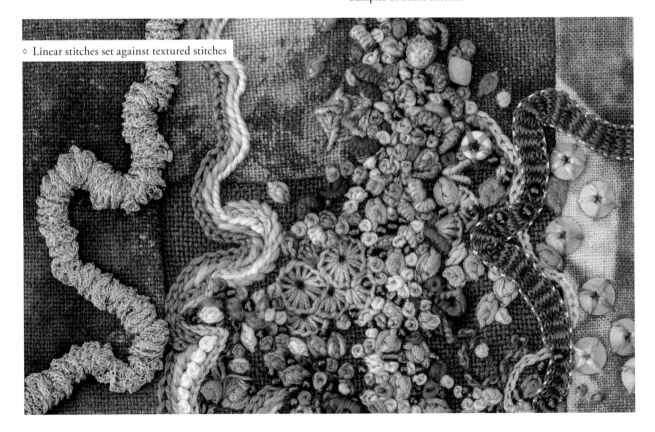

◇ Linear stitches set against textured stitches

Doubling Up

There are many designs where you can use linear stitches in two parallel lines. Give many embroidery designs a contemporary twist by simply duplicating some or all of their lines, using linear stitches. Doubling or tripling the number of lines can really enhance retro Scandinavian designs, paisley patterns, contemporary folk art, mandala designs, and Zentangle doodles.

Two lines worked side by side can add a simple, effective, modern twist. It is simple to work two parallel lines in different colors and just like that, you have an interesting piece of embroidery.

Doubling up is a really simple way to take an older design and modernize it. When you first try this technique, print out two or three copies of the pattern that you want to adapt, then take to it with a pen and draw in a few extra lines. You will see what is likely to work, and whether an extra line does what you want it to do.

The idea of duplicating a line can be demonstrated with arrow stitch (page 29)—the basic, unadorned, traditional arrow stitch.

If you work two rows of arrow stitch close together, you create a line that feels more modern, as the line is strengthened visually.

Stacking three rows makes the line even stronger. This row looks darker, despite being the same thread as used in the previous samples. This example shows how increasing the density of stitches can change the tone and visual weight. Increasing density is a play point!

The density of stitches creates a darker tone and visual weight. Blackwork is a traditional form of embroidery that uses this technique to create tones in a design. In blackwork, when a stitcher wants to create a darker area in a design, the solution is to work more stitches closer together.

A third line of stitches adds visual density, making the line stronger.

Another way to create more impact is to incorporate wider linear stitches in your design. Stitches such as double buttonhole (page 57) or reversed buttonhole bar (page 64) produce a thicker line and add more texture.

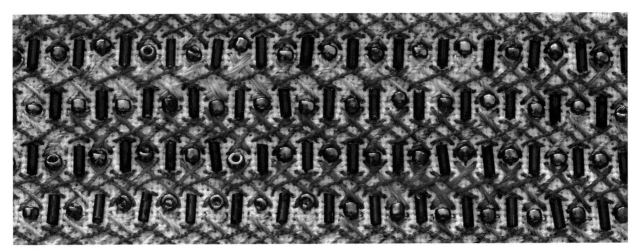

In this sample, two lines of herringbone stitch are stacked on top of each other. Stacking the lines of stitches creates a highly textured surface. Beads were added between the rows.

Pattern Making

Creating patterns is very much part of the tradition of textile design. Patterns and textiles have gone hand in hand, down through the ages. One of the greatest delights as an embroiderer, is to create patterns with needle and thread. The simple activity of covering cloth with pattern is an endless source of pleasure and experimentation.

Traditional embroidery books will often have stitches such as herringbone stitch (page 136), Cretan stitch (page 111), chevron stitch (page 100), buttonhole (page 43) or feather stitch (page 124) worked in single line. These traditional stitches can be worked in single lines, or used to fill a shape, or create part of a border. They can also be worked row upon row to build up a pattern.

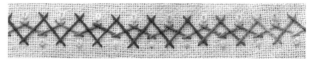

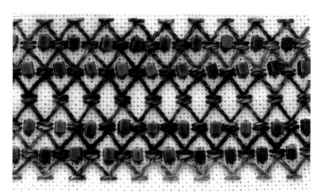

Changing the height of stitches can set up opportunities to create different patterns. Here, two rows of herringbone worked at different heights establish a pattern.

Enjoy creating patterns with stitches! This pattern consists of lines of chevron stitch worked in Caron Watercolour variegated thread. I added beads in the spaces.

Row Upon Row

You can work many stitches row upon row to create a rich surface of pattern over an area. In the last few years, models on the catwalks of Paris have displayed clothing with rich decorative surfaces, made of fabric embroidered in patterns.

Repetition is a play point and the key design element in creating patterns. When you repeat stitches in a regular manner over an area, you create a pattern. You can build up complex, interesting original designs.

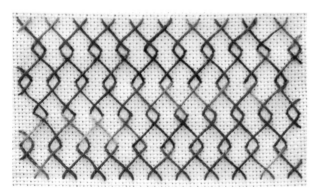

Rows of herringbone stitch creating a simple pattern; hand-dyed perle cotton #5

Rows of herringbone stitch that have been further worked by adding some beads to the spaces

Of course, some stitches are known as filling stitches. In this book, trellis stitch (page 38) is an example of a traditional filling stitch. However, many stitches work well as patterns when you stitch row upon row. Stitches such as arrow stitch (page 29), herringbone (page 136), Cretan (page 111), chevron (page 100), buttonhole (page 43), alternating buttonhole (page 45), crossed buttonhole (page 56), triangular feather stitch (page 130), triangular buttonhole (page 66), and half-chevron stitch (page 103) all create patterns when you work them row upon row.

Row-Upon-Row Height Changes

You can change the height and spacing of the stitches to establish different or varied patterns.

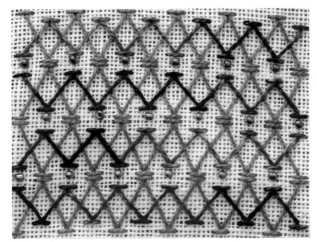

⧓ Two lines of stitches, one taller than the other, create a pattern with space for a bead.

Row-Upon-Row Arrangements

You can change the arrangement of the rows of stitches to create different patterns. You can add another dimension to your pattern-making by changing the spacing between the stitches in those rows. When you change the spacing between the stitches, it opens up small areas in the pattern where you can play with using the spaces creatively. You can easily add small isolated stitches, such French knots (page 135), detached chain stitch (page 84), oyster stitch (page 87), Algerian eye stitch (page 28), raised cross-stitch (page 118), or a small bead.

⧓ Two rows of buttonhole stitch worked face to face. By changing the height and the spacing of the stitches, I was able to add small bugle beads in the gaps. The beads create a secondary pattern.

Rows Face to Face

To easily establish a pattern, flip every second row so that the stitches are face to face or *mirrored*.

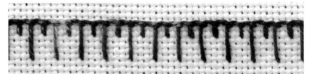

⧓ On this row of buttonhole stitch (page 43), I changed the height of every second stitch.

⧓ A second row of buttonhole stitch (page 43) in a face-to-face arrangement

Some traditional stitches already do this and have become known as a stitch variety. Double buttonhole (page 57) is an example of two rows of buttonhole, worked face to face with the second row offset.

You can combine ideas. For instance, two lines of arrow stitch (page 29) worked face to face look simple. If you use the doubling-up play point, the embroidery takes on more presence.

◇ Two lines of arrow stitch worked face to face

◇ Double lines of arrow stitch worked face to face

Rows Back to Back

Many stitches such as herringbone (page 136), chevron (page 100), Cretan (page 111), buttonhole (page 43), crossed buttonhole (page 56), triangular buttonhole (page 66), and half-chevron stitch (page 103) can easily be worked back to back to create interesting patterns.

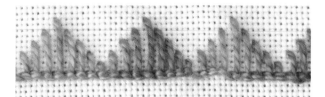

A line of buttonhole stitch where I have changed the height and spacing of the stitches to create a pattern

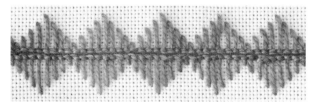

Two rows of buttonhole stitch worked in the same pattern back to back

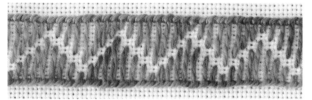

Two rows of buttonhole stitch worked in the same pattern face to face

When you work row upon row and change the spacing of the stitches, you increase the number of play points. Stitches can be worked far apart or close together. Also, when you change the spacing of a stitch, you often also change the density of the stitch. Stitches worked closer together produce darker tones.

Rows Offset

Offset a line of stitches for another play point. You can offset lines for both face-to-face rows and back-to-back rows of stitching. Rows of herringbone (page 136), chevron (page 100), Cretan (page 111), buttonhole (page 43), crossed buttonhole (page 56), triangular buttonhole (page 66), and half-chevron (page 103) work well when offset.

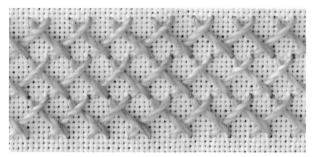

Three rows of herringbone worked in a regular manner. Compare the pattern created with the next photograph.

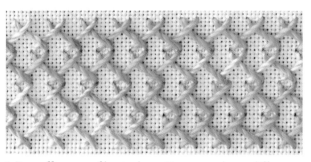

Four offset rows of herringbone. You can see how a different pattern is set up by simply working every second row offset.

Overlapped and Stacked Stitches

When you overlap or stack rows of stitches, you can create rich areas of texture and change the density of stitches. There are some traditional stitches, such as battlement stitch (page 52), that overlap each row in order to create a fill. You can also overlap stitches, such as herringbone (page 136), Cretan (page 111), and chevron (page 100).

There are a number of play points when overlapping stitches. One is to simply overlap the same-size stitch. Another play point is to change the scale of one line of stitches.

For other play points, change the scale and spacing to create interesting variations and patterns. Or work in thick and thin threads or work one row in regular thread and the second overlapping thread in a metallic thread.

Two lines of overlapped chevron stitch. The first row is a different height to the second. Two lines are worked face to face creating a secondary pattern of the spaces between the stitches. This pattern allows for an isolated stitch or bead to be added.

Chevron stitches that have been overlapped but worked at different heights. In this case, I used two threads—both are variegated but of slightly different weights.

◊ Details of stitches that are packed tightly overlapped and stacked

Free-Form

There is no rule that says you have to work on a grid. In contemporary embroidery, you can overlap stitches in a free-form manner, building up layers of color and texture. You can also stack these free-form stitches, creating texture and depth of color. If you combine a free-form stacking technique with some of the textured stitches that sit proud of the surface, such as woven trellis (page 186) or whipped wheel (page 183), the contrast adds impact.

Design Tip When building up patterns, contrast is as important as repetition. Create visual interest by contrasting your thread's color and thickness, and change the size, spacing, and angle of your stitches.

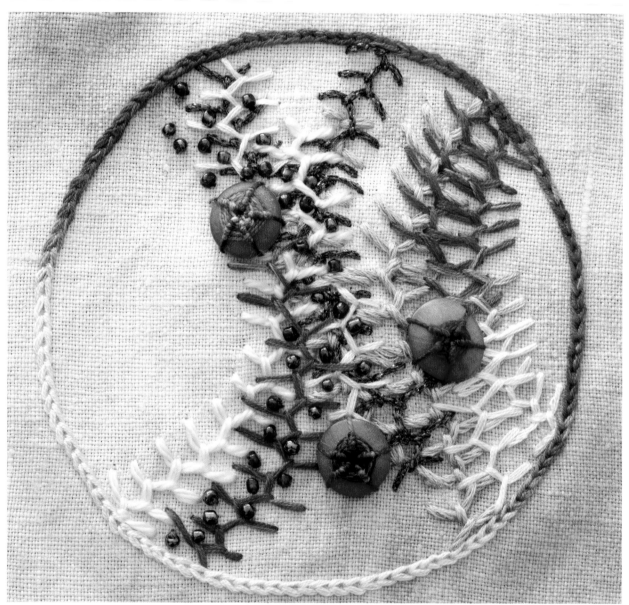

Cretan stitch (page 111) worked in a free-form style in a variety of threads, such as stranded floss, crochet cotton, and fine knitting yarn. Whipped wheel over-a-bead (page 185) are worked to create a contrast and point of interest.

Laced and Threaded Stitches

Interlacing stitches and threading a second thread through a foundation row of stitches is another play-point technique that allows you to adapt and change the look of a stitch. You can change the color, thickness or texture of the lacing thread so that the contrast can make your stitching pop.

Simple threading can be added to stitches such as backstitch (page 33), chain stitch (page 80), and running stitch (page 156). Any of the stitches that have a base or a foot, such as chevron (page 100) or buttonhole (page 43), also can be threaded.

Rows of threaded chain stitch (page 88) laced with a metallic thread. The lines between are whipped chain (page 94). Both have a foundation of chain stitch but have been treated differently.

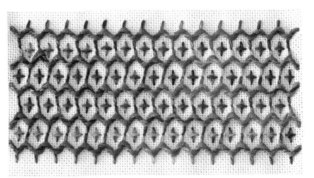

Cretan stitch worked in Caron Watercolour thread, which was then laced with tubular rayon knitting yarn. The lacing technique was adapted from twisted lattice band (page 146).

Look at how stitches are laced and threaded for ideas on adapting other stitches. For instance, the lacing used in twisted lattice band (page 146) and both versions of laced arrow stitch (pages 31 and 32) can be applied to many other stitches.

◇ Arrow stitch and laced arrow stitch worked row upon row in a variety of threads

Whipping Stitches

When you whip a stitch, it creates a slightly raised line and makes the stitch appear more clearly defined and strong. Running stitch (page 156) can also be whipped, as well as whipped backstitch (page 39), chain stitch (page 94), and stem stitch (page 171). You can also whip stitches like buttonhole wheel (page 68). Barb stitch (page 51) is made up of 2 lines of buttonhole worked back to back then whipped together.

Whipped wheel (page 183) is an isolated, highly textured stitch. When you examine the structure, you have 5 spokes radiating from a center point that are then whipped. This is a play point, as you can adapt this whipping technique to any radiating set of spokes. This means that spokes radiating from beads, sequins, and found objects such as washers can easily be whipped and incorporated into textured stitching.

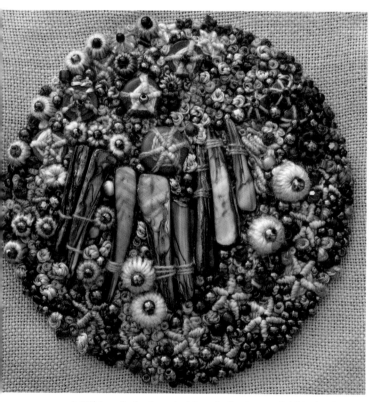

Whipped wheels and whipped wheels over disklike beads in a bed of French knots and beads. Worked in various threads of differing thicknesses.

Isolated Stitches

Isolated stitches can be used as single units or arranged in patterns and used to enhance texture. Many isolated stitches can be arranged in patterns in their own right, Stitches such as fly stitch (page 131), tulip stitch (page 91), and Algerian eye stitch (page 28) all have possibilities. Knotted stitches, such as French knot (page 135), bullion knot (page 41), and of course, buttonhole wheels (page 68) and whipped wheels (page 183), can also become points of emphasis.

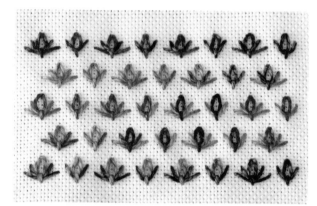

A pattern created by using isolated stitches. Tulip stitch (page 91) is worked in Caron Watercolour thread.

◊ A few isolated stitches add interest to fabric collage

Adding a Fringe

Adding a fringe to the base of your stitches is a play point that can be heaps of fun! You can add a fringe to any stitch that has a base line or a foot. For some reason, when a stitch lifts from the surface of the fabric, it makes people smile and want to touch it. Adding a fringe does this.

If you want to experiment with adding fringing to stitches, take a look at fringed chevron stitch (page 102) and fringed button-hole stitch (page 58), and think about trying the technique with stitches such as backstitch (page 33), buttonhole wheel (page 68), and half-chevron stitch (page 103). Look at the structure of the stitch for a loop from which to hang the fringe threads.

Fringing at the base line of buttonhole stitch (page 43) creates these abstract flowers. This motif has been worked in hand-dyed silk that is the same thickness as perle cotton #8.

Other Ways to Change a Stitch—Use Different Threads!

Have fun with different threads. Many stitches look a bit flat if you use mainly stranded cotton floss. Try some threads with a firmer twist, to bulk out a stitch with more body. Threads are available in all sizes, thick and thin, shiny and dull, smooth and lumpy, and using a variety adds plenty of interest to stitching.

Don't be afraid to try a thread that is not technically an embroidery thread, such as a fine knitting yarn. If the thread will go through the eye of a needle, at least try to stitch with it, as you never know what discoveries you will make. There are many interesting knitting yarns. Do not dismiss them. If you can't stitch with it, you can always couch it down, so you have not lost anything.

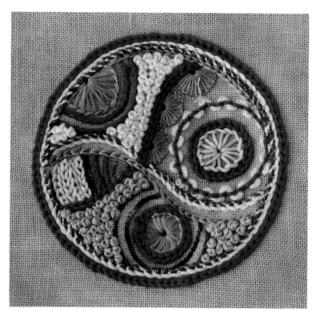

This piece contains stranded cotton floss, perle cotton #8, perle cotton #5, acrylic knitting yarn, crotchet cotton, and metallic thread.

When selecting thread, I also aim for a contrast of texture and color. If I am stacking stitches, working one row on top of another, or layering a stitch, I always think about changing the thread, as it can lead to interesting contrasts.

Simple linear stitches in a contemporary design. Some of the effect in varying the line is created by using different weights of perle cotton #5 and #8.

Ask Questions and Find the Play Points

There are many play points to be found while stitching. It can be fun to spot how many play points you can discover. When you look at stitches, think about how they might be arranged to do more for you. You might want a stronger line, or to fill an area. Think about how stitches can be layered, duplicated, flipped, and changed. Whenever you encounter a stitch, break up the steps and ask yourself if this is a point in the process that you can explore and play with the stitch. Some of these questions may help you find the play points as you explore them out on a doodle cloth.

- How does this stitch behave on a curve?

- Can I work this stitch in a circle? In a triangle? In a square? As a diamond?

- What happens if you work row upon row?

- What happens if I add beads?

- Can two rows of this stitch be worked mirrored face to face?

- Can rows be offset from each other?

- Can two rows of this stitch be worked back to back?

- What happens if you overlap the rows?

- Can you overlap and offset the rows to make a different pattern?

- Can you change the size of each overlapped row?

- Can this stitch be laced with another thread?

- Can this stitch be whipped?

- Can this stitch or parts of this stitch be woven?

- What happens if you change the spacing of this stitch?

- Can you change the scale of parts of the stitch?

- Which parts of the stitch can you make bigger or smaller?

- Can you make some parts of the row large and some parts small?

- What happens if you use thin or thicker thread?

- What happens if you work one row in thick thread and one row in thin thread?

- What happens if you work blocks of rows changing to different colored threads?

- What happens if I stitch beyond the frame or pattern?

These are just a few questions you can ask yourself and to prompt ideas for play points as you stitch. Now on with the stitches!

◇ Creative embroidery monotone panel

The Stitches

Algerian Eye Stitch

Algerian eye stitch is traditionally worked on even-weave fabric. You see this stitch used in canvas work, pulled work, embroidery, and forms of counted-thread work. Using different arrangements of Algerian eye stitch, it is very easy to build up interesting designs, motifs, and patterns. It is also known as the *star stitch* because it creates a starlike pattern if turned on its point.

Tip If you want to use Algerian eye on regular dress fabric, use waste canvas to achieve even stitches.

Work each straight stitch into the center hole by bringing your needle out on the edge of the stitch and taking it back down into the central hole.

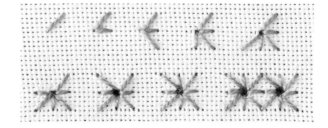

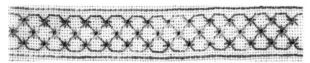

◊ Algerian eye scattered across an area of satin stitch (page 161)

◊ Lines of half-Algerian eye stitches turned on point

◊ Algerian eye worked in a border alongside backstitch (page 33)

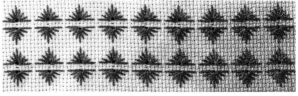

§ A border pattern of Algerian eye stitches that have been turned on point and with 1 stitch omitted on each side

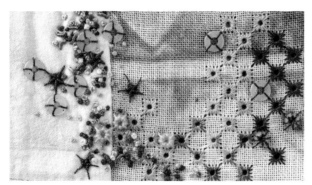

§ Free-form Algerian eye with French knots (page 135), bullion knots (page 41), whipped wheels (page 183), and beads

§ Algerian eye stitches turned on their point and outlined in backstitch (page 33). These are combined with satin stitch (page 161).

Arrow Stitch

You can create different varieties of this stitch by simply working it in different directions. Both horizontal and vertical varieties are quick, easy stitches that swiftly build into a simple border pattern. The geometric structure allows you to create numerous patterns with different arrangements.

Horizontal Arrow Stitch

1. Work a diagonal stitch between 2 imaginary horizontal lines. Bring the thread out on the bottom line.

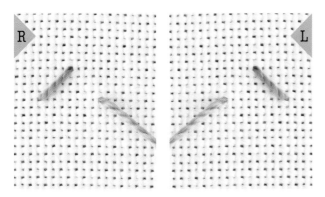

2. Go up to the top line and take a bite of the fabric.

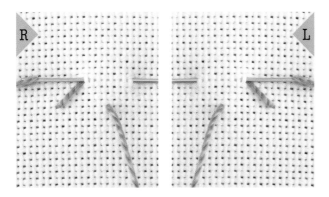

3. Work along the line in a zigzag fashion.

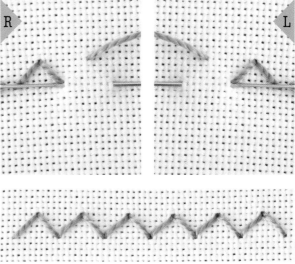

◊ Horizontal arrow stitch

Vertical Arrow Stitch

1. Working between 2 imaginary vertical lines, make 2 straight stitches in a V formation.

2. Bring the thread out just below the first V and pass the needle behind the first 2 stitches.

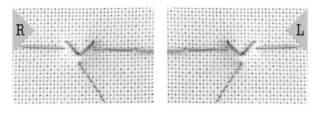

3. Continue building the pattern as you work down the line.

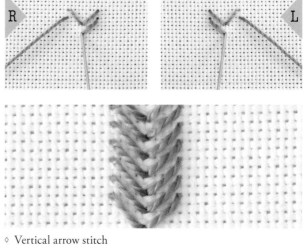

◇ Vertical arrow stitch

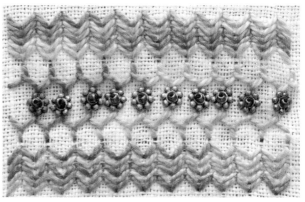

◇ Work row upon row to build patterns.

◇ Arrow stitch is combined with 2 rows of Cretan stitch (page 111) worked back to back.

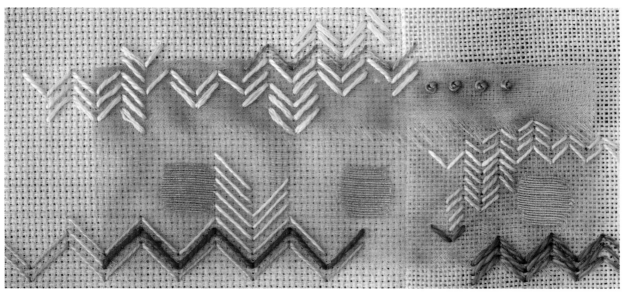

◇ Free-form vertical and horizontal arrow stitches

Arrow Stitch (Laced 1)

You can lace arrow stitch in a number of ways that are quick and easy to work. This version of laced arrow stitch is so simple it can be easily taught to children.

Work a foundation row of horizontal arrow stitch. Then weave a second thread through the foundation stitches.

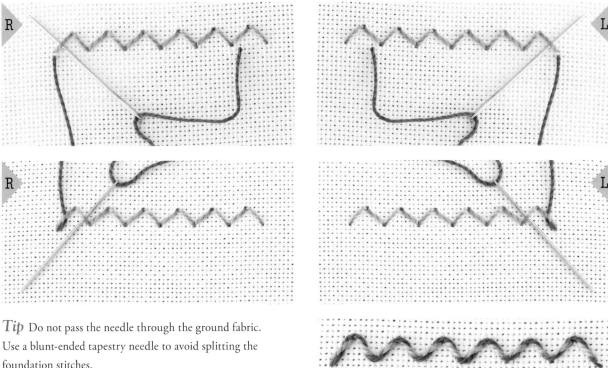

Tip Do not pass the needle through the ground fabric. Use a blunt-ended tapestry needle to avoid splitting the foundation stitches.

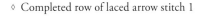

◇ Completed row of laced arrow stitch 1

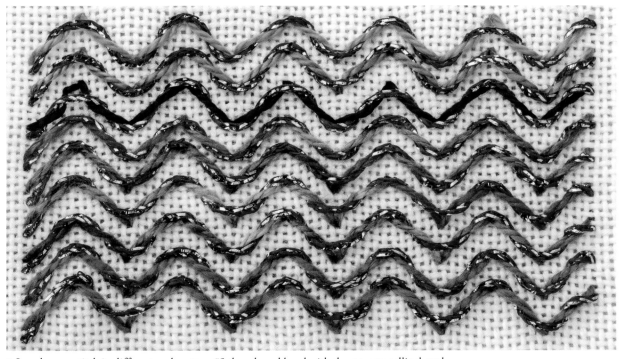

◇ Laced arrow stitch in different perle cotton #5 threads and laced with the same metallic thread.

Arrow Stitch (Laced 2)

Laced arrow stitch 2 creates a braidlike appearance which makes an ideal border. This stitch looks interesting if you experiment and lace with thicker yarn and novelty threads.

1. Work a foundation row of horizontal arrow stitch.

2. To lace a second thread, bring your thread out on the bottom line. Pass the needle under the second diagonal stitch.

Tip Use a blunt-ended tapestry needle for the second thread so you do not split the foundation threads as you sew.

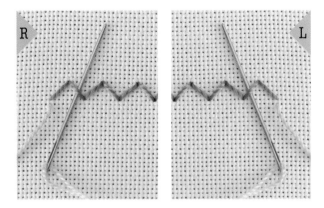

3. Take the thread under the first diagonal stitch.

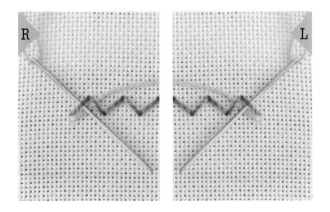

4. Moving from peak to valley, lace the line of stitches. As you lace, make sure you keep the lacing thread under the needle.

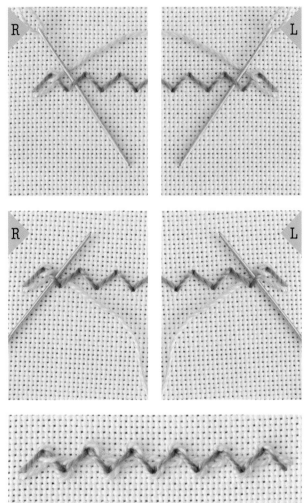

◇ A completed line of laced arrow stitch 2

◇ Two sets of laced arrow stitch 2 worked in a border pattern

Backstitch

Backstitch is a good, basic linear stitch that forms a clean line in a design. Backstitch can be used as a delicate outline or as a foundation in composite stitches, such as Pekinese stitch (page 151). If you want to give blackwork patterns a modern twist, work the design in backstitch using over-dyed or variegated threads.

1. If needed, mark your line with a quilter's pencil or soluble pen or pencil. Bring the thread up from the back of the fabric and make a backward stitch. Bring the needle out on the line, a little in front of the first stitch.

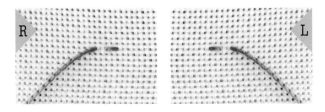

2. Make the second stitch backward, inserting the needle into the hole made by the first stitch. Bring the needle out in front of the second stitch. Repeat this back-and-forth movement along the line.

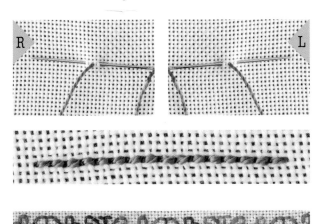

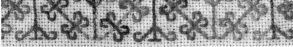

A traditional blackwork pattern worked in backstitch in a hand-dyed variegated silk thread

◇ A traditional blackwork pattern worked in a variegated thread

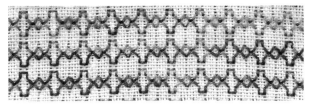

Blackwork patterns can create fills that echo a traditional feel but are light and airy.

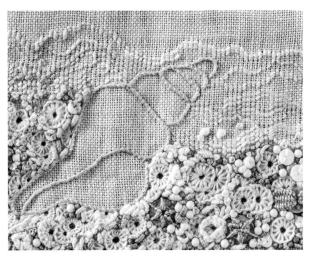

Set against the highly textured embroidery, the simple backstitch defines the lines of sand and creates an interesting contrast in the design. I worked multiple lines in similar-toned threads but with different thicknesses and textures.

Backstitch worked through the holes of the Heishi beads, which are small disks of shell. They usually have a large-ish hole, which makes them ideal to include in your stitching projects.

Backstitch (Beaded)

Beaded backstitch is simply a line of backstitch (page 33), to which you add a bead on every second stitch.

You can create interesting designs by adding the bead every third or fourth stitch and so on. It is up to you and is part of the fun beading this stitch.

You also can add other stitching techniques, such as weaving a secondary thread under the backstitches.

Use a tapestry #26 needle. It is fine enough to thread a bead, yet the eye is wide enough to take a perle cotton #8.

1. Bring the thread up on the line that you want to create and make a small backward stitch. Bring the needle through the fabric a little in front of the first stitch and still on the line.

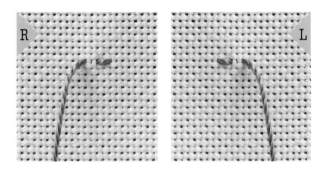

2. Thread a bead and make the second stitch.

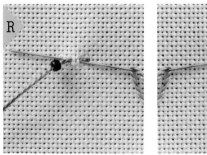

3. Continue the pattern of a regular backstitch followed by a beaded backstitch.

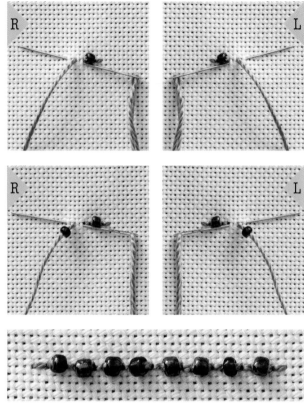

◊ A completed line of beaded backstitch

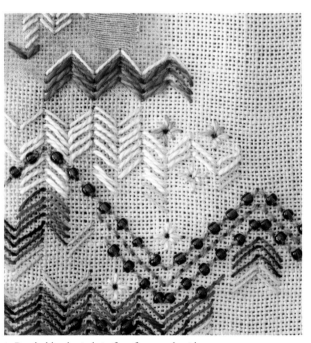

◊ Beaded backstitch in free-form embroidery

Backstitch (Threaded)

Threaded backstitch creates a decorative line that is quick and easy to work, as it is simply a laced version of basic backstitch (page 33). This means the threaded variation will have the same linear qualities as backstitch—it can hold a curve well or be an outline, for example.

Combinations of basic backstitch and threaded backstitch worked row upon row look good together. Whenever you see a stitch that has two parts to its construction, often you can change the thread on the second part of the process—it can be a different color, different thickness, or texture. Any of these changes can add interest and variety to your embroidery.

1. Work a foundation row of backstitch. Make each stitch slightly longer and looser than usual to accommodate the thread you will weave under them.

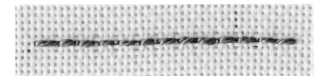

2. Use a blunt-ended tapestry needle to weave a second thread, alternating up and down under the row of backstitches. Pass the needle under the foundation stitches without entering the fabric.

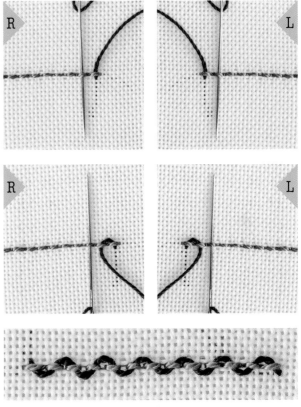

◇ The finished threaded backstitch

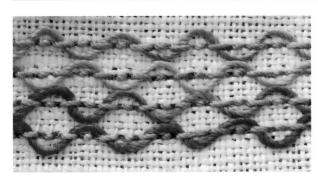

§ I worked the foundation backstitches in perle cotton #5 and threaded them with a hand-dyed silk thread.

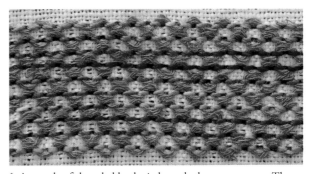

§ A sample of threaded backstitch worked row upon row. The foundation of backstitches is worked in hand-dyed variegated silk that is the thickness of perle cotton #8. It was laced with a fine chainette knitting yarn.

Backstitch (Threaded Stacked)

Threaded stacked backstitch becomes a thick line of stitching. You use the threading technique on 3 or 4 rows of backstitch or make a thick dramatic line of 10 or 12 rows of backstitch. The number of rows you can stack is limited only by the length of your needle.

You can use this stitch as a border as it will prevent fraying. Items such as table runners and place mats look good with this stitch as a simple border. You can also use it to edge projects, such as fabric postcards or the pages of fabric books.

You can vary this stitch in a number of ways, as you have the choice of lacing in one direction or both. You can change the color and texture of the yarn you use to thread the backstitches and you can work the backstitches in different colors too!

1. Work 2 or more foundation rows of backstitch. Make each stitch slightly longer and looser than usual, to accommodate the weaving thread.

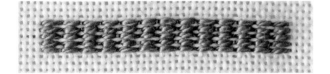

2. Use a blunt-ended tapestry needle to weave a second thread, alternating up and down under the row of backstitches. Do not pick up the fabric as you work.

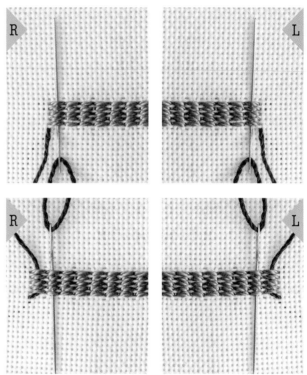

3. Continue lacing to the end of the line.

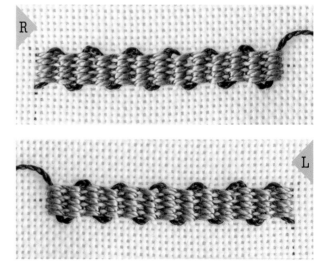

4. Turn your work and weave back along the line. Turning your work makes it easier to handle.

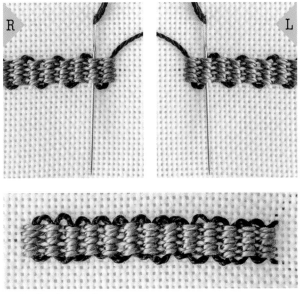

◊ The finished stitch

◊ Threaded stacked backstitch used in crazy quilting

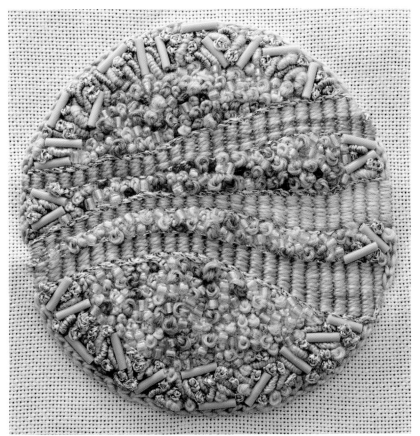

This sample was made with a foundation of 10 rows of backstitch worked in a hand-dyed perle cotton #5. The rows were threaded with a metallic thread.

Threaded stacked backstitch worked in variegated perle cotton #8

Foundation rows of backstitch, worked in a hand-dyed perle cotton #5, were laced with a metallic knitting yarn. French knots (page 135), bullion knots (page 41), seed beads, and bugle beads fill the other areas.

Backstitch (Trellis Stitch)

Trellis stitch is a traditional filling stitch consisting of a grid of backstitches worked diagonally. It creates a very attractive, quick, easily worked filling. Because it works up quickly, it is ideal for covering large areas. There are many stitches that, if you work them in a diagonal line, will create a different pattern.

1. Create the first layer of the grid by working backstitch (page 33) in diagonal parallel lines. Space the lines a stitch apart.

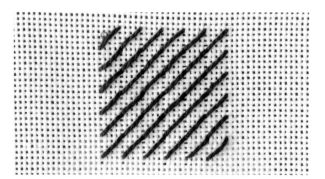

2. Add diagonal lines angled in the opposite direction. Work your backstitches at right angles and into the previous holes created when you created the first set of lines.

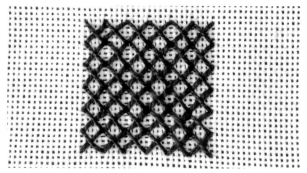

Tip If you are working an uneven shape, use partial backstitches at the edge of the shape.

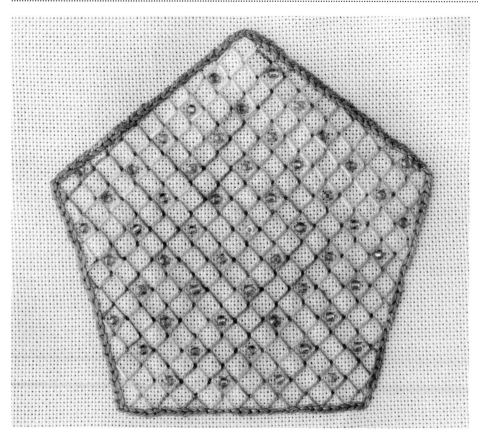

In this sample, I worked the trellis in a hand-dyed perle cotton #8 and then added seed beads. I finished with a chain stitch outline worked in the same hand-dyed cotton thread.

Backstitch (Whipped)

Whipped backstitch creates a slightly raised line that you can use in many situations. If you use a heavy thread in the same color as the foundation stitching, the line will look like a fine cord. This is a particularly useful stitch if you need a raised line on a delicate, fine fabric that will not accept a heavy thread through the weave.

1. Work a foundation row of backstitches (page 33). Make each stitch slightly longer and looser than usual so you can pass a second thread under them easily.

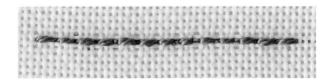

2. Use a blunt-ended tapestry needle so you will not split the foundation threads. To whip the row, bring the needle up from the back of the fabric, take the thread over the top of the backstitches and pass the needle under the first backstitch. Do not pick up any of the fabric. Pull the thread through.

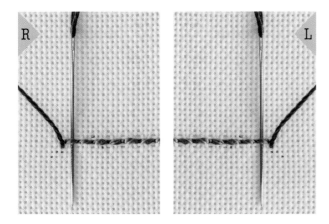

3. Repeat along the row.

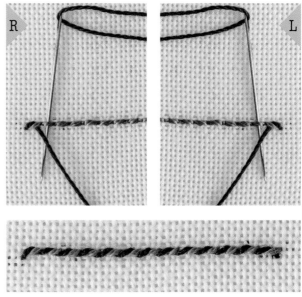

◇ A line of whipped backstitch

Basque Stitch

As the name suggests, Basque stitch is found on old embroideries from the Basque region of northern Spain, Portugal, and southern France. It is a variety of twisted chain stitch (page 93) that creates a line of twisted loops which look good on a curved line. Once you get the rhythm of this stitch, it is very relaxing and enjoyable to work.

1. Working along 2 imaginary horizontal lines, bring the thread out on the upper line, move over slightly and take a large bite of the fabric so that the needle emerges on the lower line. Take your thread across the needle, then loop the thread under the needle point.

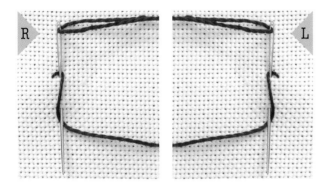

2. Pull the needle through to form a twisted loop.

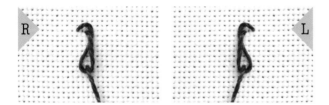

3. Insert the needle on the lower line to catch the loop down and have the needle tip emerge beside the top of the loop.

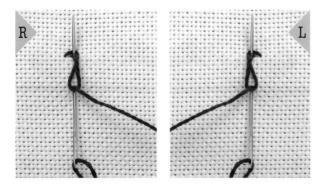

4. Take the needle through the fabric and repeat this process along the lines.

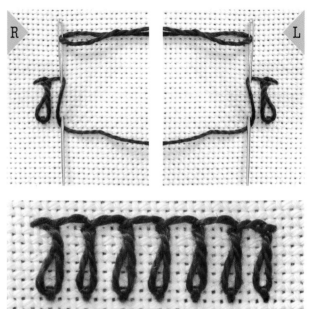

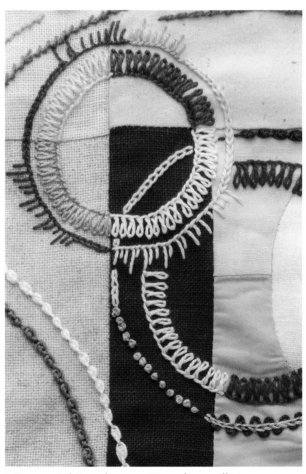

◇ Basque stitch in perle cotton #5, used in a wall piece

Bullion Knot

Tips

- Use a milliner's or straw needle. These have the same width for both the eye and the shaft, which makes it easier to slide the wrapped bullion knot along the needle.

- Wrap the thread in a clockwise direction. For most threads, this means you will follow the direction of the natural twist in which it was spun.

- If your thread untwists as you wrap the bullion, it means the thread was spun in the opposite direction to most threads on the market. In this case, wrap your bullion counterclockwise.

- If you have trouble with stranded threads getting tangled, try a twisted thread, such as perle cotton #8 or #5.

- Stretch the fabric in a needlework hoop or frame so that you have both hands free to work the knot.

- When you start to use bullion knots in your embroidery, start with a simple 4- or 5-wrap bullion. After you master those, add more wraps.

1. Bring the thread from the back of the fabric and insert the needle a short space away. Have the needle tip emerge near the place that the thread comes out of the fabric. The distance between these 2 points determines the length of the knot.

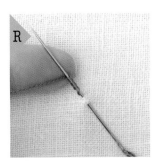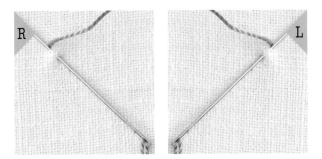

2. Wrap the thread around the needle 5 or 6 times. Do not cross the wraps on the needle; make sure the thread coils up the needle. The coil of thread on the needle should be the same distance as where the needle emerges and exits the fabric.

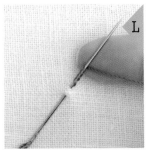

3. Gently start to pull the thread through, holding the coil between your first finger and thumb. This grip on the coil will keep the bullion knot smooth and prevent it from knotting in on itself. Pull the working thread up and away from you.

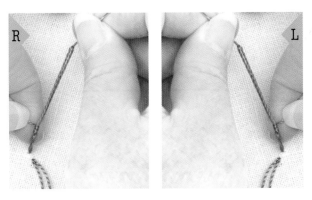

4. As the coil tightens, change direction and pull the thread toward you.

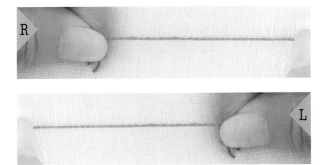

4. If the bullion bunches or looks untidy, pass the needle under the bullion and rub it up and down the length of the bullion to smooth the coils out. Stitchers call this "rubbing the belly" of the bullion.

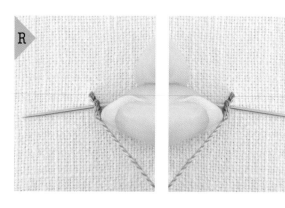

5. Take the needle through the fabric at the point where the thread first emerged. The coil of thread which is the bullion knot should now lie neatly on the surface.

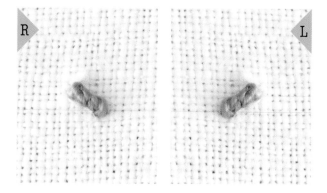

◊ Bullion knots worked in crazy quilting

Buttonhole Stitch (*also* Blanket Stitch)

Buttonhole stitch—or *blanket stitch* as many people call it—is actually the foundation stitch for a whole family of stitches. This stitch is often used along the edge of projects such as blankets—hence the name. Buttonhole is marvelously versatile, as it can be worked in a regular or free-form manner, row upon row or with rows stacked on top of each other, to create pattern and texture. This is an ideal stitch to explore changing the spacing and height of the arms and to experiment with the spacing.

1. Work from left to right (right to left for left-handed) along 2 imaginary horizontal lines. Bring the thread out on the lower line. Move to the right and make a vertical stitch, from upper line to lower line, looping the working thread under the needle point. Pull the thread through.

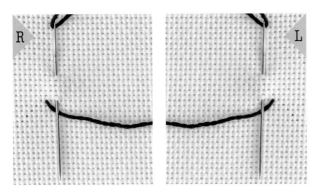

2. Repeat along the line.

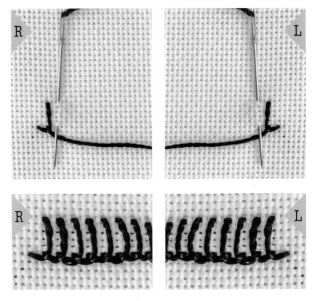

A detail of a larger wall piece. Buttonhole with arms worked at an irregular height follow and emphasize linear stitches, such as stem stitch (page 167) and chain stitch (page 80).

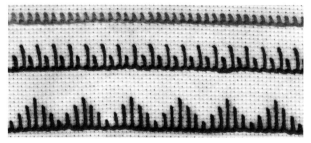

§ You can create many interesting patterns with this stitch.
§ By varying the arm length, you can create shapes.

§ Build up interesting bands by working buttonhole stitch back
§ to back, changing the height of the arms to create patterns.

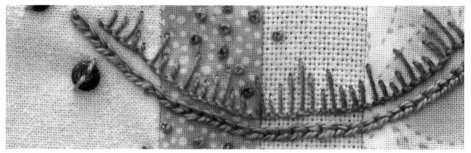

§ Buttonhole follows a curve well. In this example, buttonhole in hand-dyed perle cotton #5 follows
§ and emphasizes a line of chain stitch (page 80) worked in the same thread.

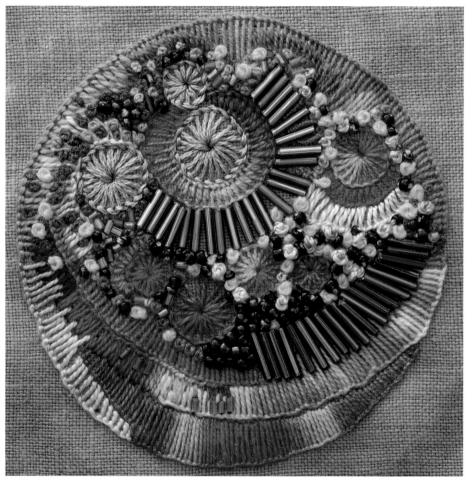

§ Free-form buttonhole stitches worked in a variety of threads combined with buttonhole wheels
§ (page 68), French knots (page 135), seed beads, and bugle beads

Buttonhole Stitch (Alternating)

Alternating buttonhole is a versatile variety of buttonhole stitch (page 43), worked so the stitches fall to each side of a central spine.

This is a great stitch with which to explore creating patterns, as it is easy to vary the number of stitches, the height of each stitch, and the spacing of each stitch on each side of the central line. You can develop numerous patterns by simply working row upon row. If the rows of alternating buttonhole are offset, you have more options.

Alternating buttonhole is quick and easy to work and follows a curve well. You can also work alternating buttonhole in an irregular manner, producing an organic twiglike line.

1. Work 3 or 4 buttonhole stitches (page 43).

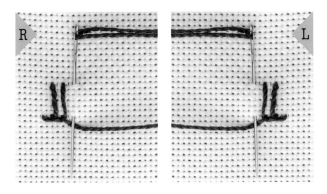

2. Make the next set of stitches on the other side of the central line.

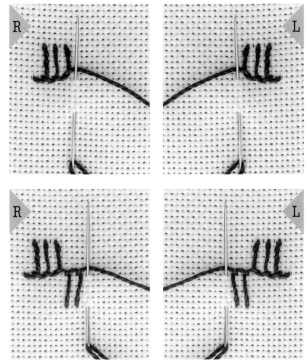

3. Repeat the pattern.

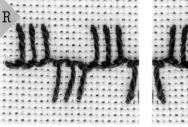
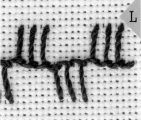

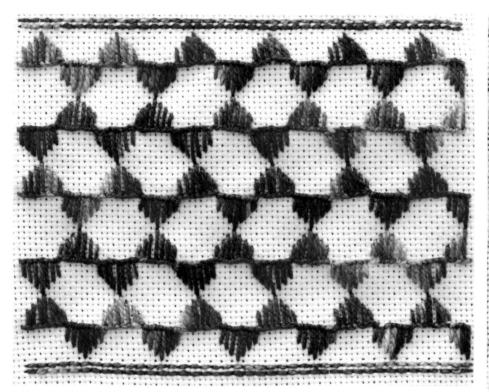

◇ Rows of alternating buttonhole in a hand-dyed perle cotton #8

◊ Alternating buttonhole with the "arms" at an angle and beads added later

◇ Alternating buttonhole worked free-form on a crazy quilt block

Buttonhole Stitch (Alternating Up-and-Down)

Alternating up-and-down buttonhole can be worked in a regular or free-form manner. It looks good worked row upon row and leaves wide spaces into which you can stitch a bead. If you work it free form, it creates an interesting twiggy line that is ideal for small floral motifs.

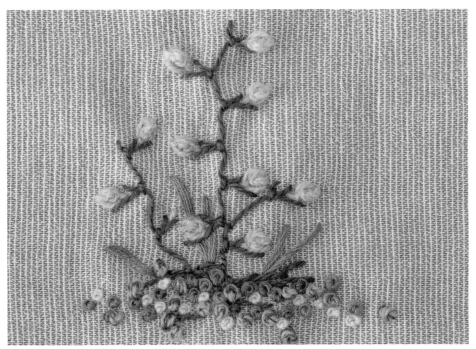

⸖ Free-form alternating up-and-down buttonhole stitch in perle cotton #8. Oyster stitch (page 87)
⸖ in wool forms the buds. French knots (page 135) in wool make up the base.

1. Start with a buttonhole stitch (page 43).

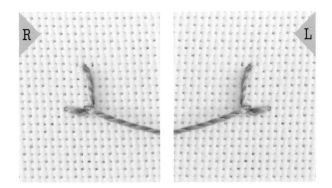

2. For the second part of the stitch, insert the needle and take a bite of the fabric so that the tip of the needle is pointing up.

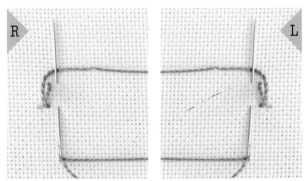

3. Wrap the working thread under the needle and pull the needle through the fabric. Pull the needle toward you instead of away from you. Hold down the loop that forms with the opposite thumb to prevent it slipping. This loop forms the bar at the base of both stitches.

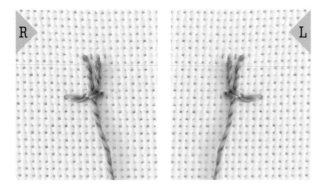

4. Work the next pair of stitches pointing in the other direction.

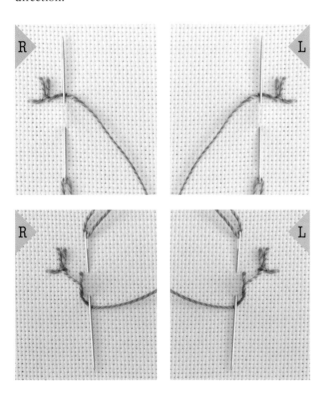

5. Continue along the line, alternating the direction of each pair of stitches.

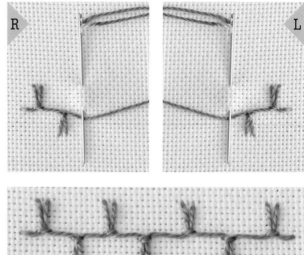

◊ A line of alternating up-and-down buttonhole

⧘ Alternating up-and-down buttonhole stitch worked in a relaxed manner on a crazy quilt block

Buttonhole Stitch (Bar)

Buttonhole bar is often used in traditional pulled and drawn needlework. It forms a loop that stands clear of the foundation fabric. You can use it to create loops to lace ribbon under or to loop around a button, but it is not just a utilitarian stitch.

If you use buttonhole bar in a contemporary free-form manner, you soon discover this stitch is interesting, fun, and highly addictive! Hand-dyed multicolored threads can look interesting, as with this type of thread the color shifts along the bar.

Tips

• It's important to keep your tension even, so stretch the fabric in a needlework hoop or frame while you work.

• As you learn this stitch, use a thread such perle cotton #8 or #5. When you have mastered it, experiment with other threads.

• Use a blunt-ended tapestry needle for the second thread so you do not split the foundation threads as you sew.

1. Using a firm thread, start with 2 or 3 horizontal straight stitches across the area you wish the bar to lay. This forms the bar on which you sew.

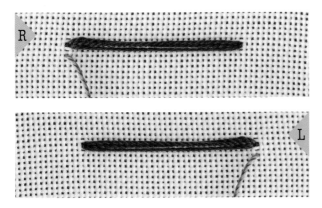

2. Starting at the lower left (or right, for left-handed) side, work a buttonhole stitch (page 43) over the bar of straight stitches. Do not pass the needle through the fabric, just under the bar. As you work, nudge the stitches along the bar so that they are snug, but not so tight they twist the bar.

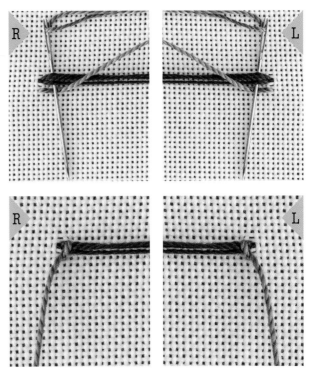

3. At the end of the bar, take your needle to the back and secure it.

A free-form sample of buttonhole bar worked in a piece of highly textured embroidery

◊ Buttonhole bar is used for the sepals at the tops of the blackberries. It is worked in hand-dyed silk thread the same thickness as
◊ perle cotton #8.

Buttonhole Stitch (var. Barb Stitch)

Barb stitch is a traditional buttonhole stitch worked back to back and then whipped with a second thread. You can work barb stitch either straight in a single line or on a curve. When worked in an irregular curve, it looks very organic. The whipping stitches create a slightly raised line along the center.

If you work barb stitch in a straight line, you can vary the height of the arms to create a huge variety of patterns. You can work row upon row or offset the lines to create patterns. Different arrangements of the rows can build up interlocking patterns to create interesting fillings.

1. Work 2 rows of buttonhole stitch (page 43) back to back.

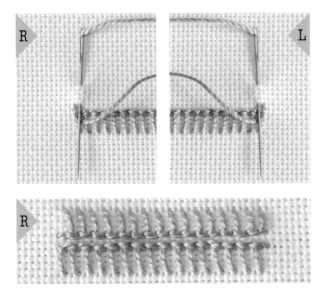

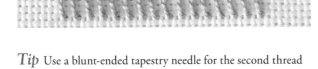

Tip Use a blunt-ended tapestry needle for the second thread so you do not split the foundation threads as you sew.

§ Barb stitch in perle cotton #5, with French knots (page 135)
§ in over-dyed cotton stranded floss

2. Using a second thread, slide the needle under each loop at the base of the buttonhole and pull the thread through so that you whip the 2 rows of buttonhole together.

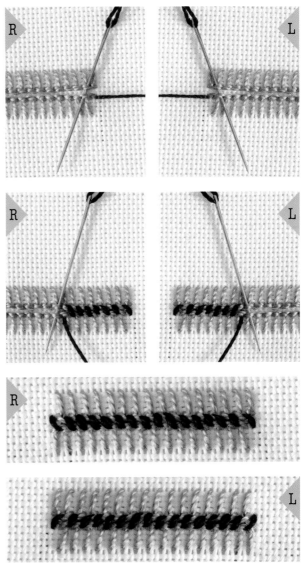

Buttonhole Stitch (*var. Battlement Stitch*)

Battlement stitch is traditionally stacked row upon row. The overlapping lines create a thick solid border or fill.

Like regular buttonhole stitch, you can create many interesting patterns by varying the height of the stitches on the first row. You can also work this stitch in a nontraditional, free-form manner.

You can change many simple stitches into areas of rich texture by using this stacking technique. Try it with herringbone (page 136), chevron (page 100), fly stitch (page 131), Cretan (page 111), and other varieties.

1. Work a line of buttonhole stitches (page 43).

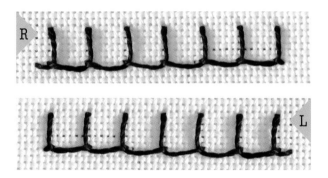

2. To start the second journey, bring your needle out just below the first row base line. Insert your needle, stepped down and to the right on the upper line.

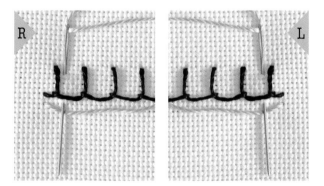

3. Work another line of buttonhole stitches, each stitch stepped down and to the right.

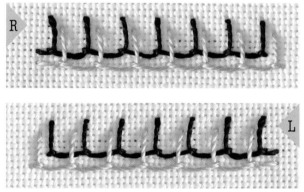

4. Work a third row, also stepped down and the right.

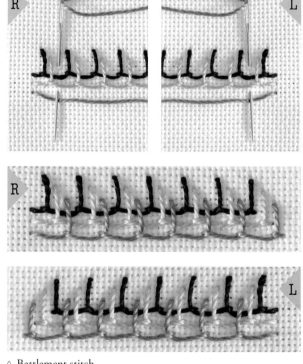

◇ Battlement stitch

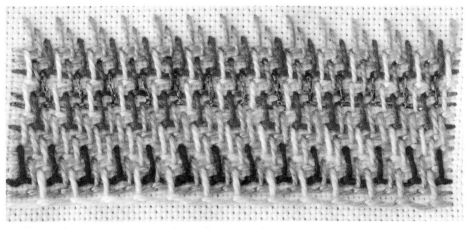

◇ A block of battlement stitch worked in different threads

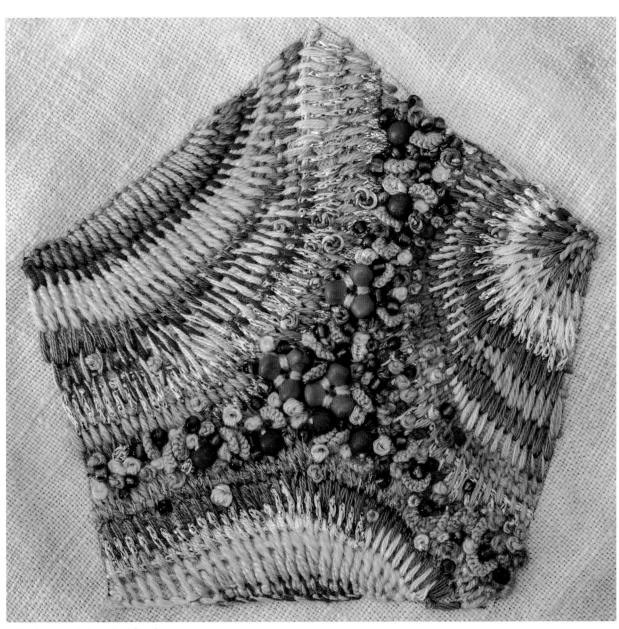

◇ Battlement stitch worked free-form

Buttonhole Stitch (Beaded)

Beaded buttonhole is fun version of regular buttonhole stitch (page 43) and there are a lot of varieties of buttonhole to which you can apply this technique. Here, the beading is done *during* the stitching process—*not* added afterward.

With this stitch you can change where and when you add beads, the height of the arms, and the spacing to create different patterns. The combinations are endless.

Tip You can bead most stitches. The trick is to use a tapestry #26 needle. Since the eye of a tapestry needle is long, you can thread perle cotton #8 and #5 through the long eye. However, the needle itself is thin, which means you can add a bead to your working thread as you stitch.

1. Work a couple of regular buttonhole stitches.

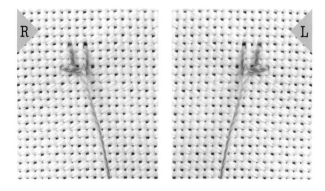

2. Thread 3 or 4 seed beads or a bugle bead on your working thread and make another buttonhole stitch, starting high enough to accommodate the beads.

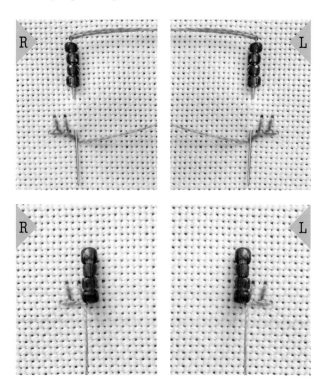

3. Repeat this pattern, adding beads on every third arm along the line.

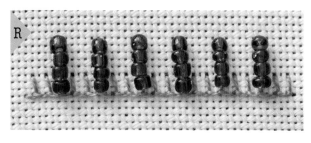

◊ A line of beaded buttonhole

Buttonhole Stitch (Closed)

Closed buttonhole stitch is easily worked, quick to build, and holds a curve very well. It can be used as an alternative to basic buttonhole stitch and as an edging. It can be used to couch a ribbon, braid, or novelty thread to your work. Since it has a strong geometric structure, it is also ideal to use in multiple rows to create a patterned border or filling.

1. Work over 2 imaginary parallel lines, or mark 2 lines on the fabric using a water-soluble or fade-out fabric marker.

2. Bring the thread out on the lower line, insert the needle slightly to the right on the upper line, and bring the needle back near the original entry. With the thread looped under the needle point, pull the needle through the fabric.

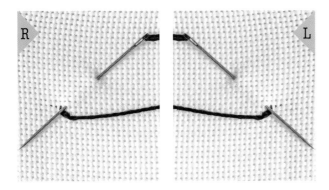

3. On the top line, insert the needle at the top of the stitch you just created. Take it diagonally to the right and bring it out on the bottom line. With the thread looped under the needle point, pull the needle through. This forms the first triangle of closed buttonhole.

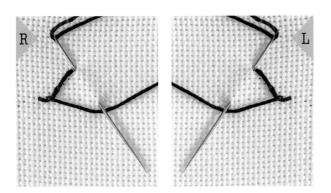

4. Continue the pattern along the line.

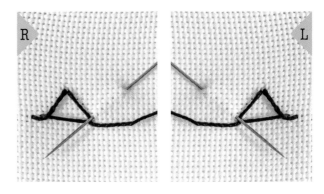

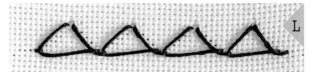

◊ A row of closed buttonhole stitch

Closed buttonhole stitches worked back to back on a curve in a free-form manner. This produces a line that has an organic feel. I added French knots (page 135), detached chain stitch (page 84), cast-on stitch (page 78), and a few small wooden beads. The threads are hand-dyed silk the same thickness as perle cotton #8.

Two rows of closed buttonhole worked back to back in a hand-dyed silk thread.

Buttonhole Stitch (Crossed)

You can use crossed buttonhole stitch to create patterns and interesting borders. It consists of pairs of angled buttonhole stitches which are crossed. You can change the spacing between the pairs of stitches or lengthen the arms. Work evenly and row upon row to create patterns. You can also use this stitch to couch on textured threads.

1. Work between 2 imaginary horizontal lines. Bring the thread out on the lower line and insert at an angle. Loop the thread under the needle point.

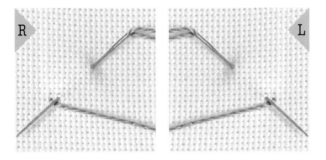

2. Pull the needle through to form the first stitch. Insert the needle at an angle, to the left (right) of the first stitch. Loop the working thread under the needle point and pull the needle through the fabric to cross the previous stitch.

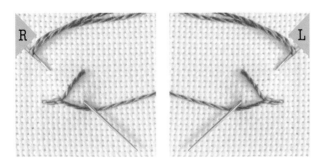

3. Repeat along the line.

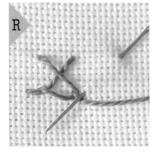
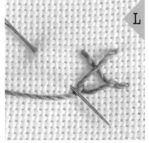

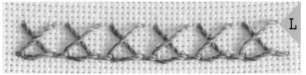

◇ A line of crossed buttonhole stitches

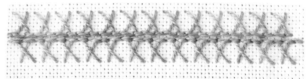

◇ Crossed buttonhole stitch worked back to back

◇ You can stack crossed buttonhole using the same technique as the battlement stitch (page 52).

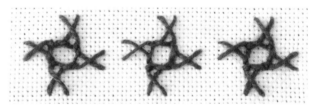

◇ Crossed buttonhole worked in a square

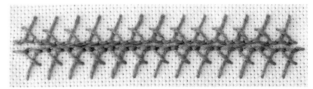

◇ Two rows of crossed buttonhole worked back to back. The first stitch of the cross was lengthened.

Buttonhole Stitch (Double)

Double buttonhole stitch is a traditional stitch simply made from 2 lines of buttonhole stitch (page 43) worked face to face. It is ideal to use along the edge of projects. It can be worked row upon row and is an easy stitch with which to experiment and explore changing the spacing and height of the arms. It also follows a curve well.

1. Start with a line of buttonhole stitches (page 43).

2. Turn your work and work a line of buttonhole stitches offset by a thread or two, so that the arms of the stitch sit in the spaces created by the first line of buttonhole stitches.

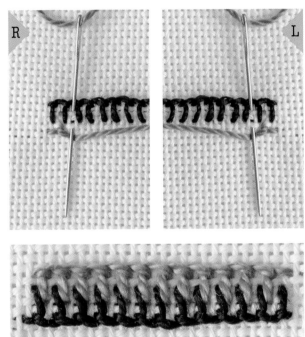

I used different colored thread to demonstrate how the stitch is worked, but usually you would use the same thread.

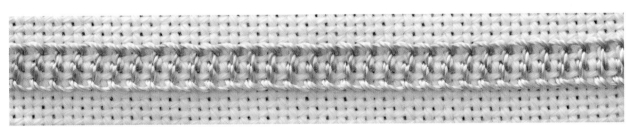

◇ Double buttonhole stitch worked in rayon thread

Buttonhole Stitch (Fringed)

Fringing adds an element of surprise to your stitches. Buttonhole is ideal for fringing because it has a baseline that easily allows for a fringe to be added.

1. Work a line of buttonhole stitch (page 43).

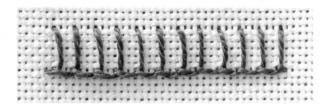

2. Cut 2 or 3 threads into lengths of about 2″–4″ (5–10 cm) and lay them together. Fold them in half. With a crochet hook, pick up the threads at the halfway point and hook them under the stitch.

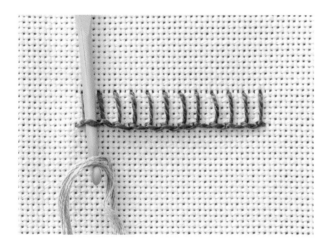

3. Pull a loop under the base of the stitch.

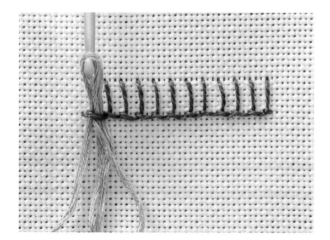

4. Fold the loop over the foundation stitch and pull the tail through the loop.

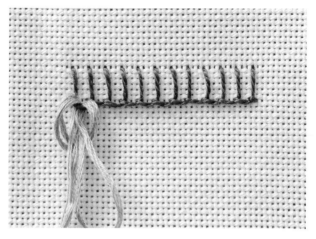

5. Pull the tail gently until the loop sits neatly on the foundation stitch.

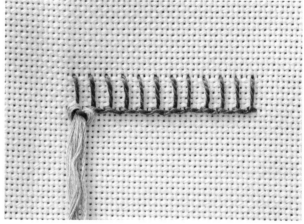

6. Continue along the line. Trim the fringe last, as that way you will get it straight.

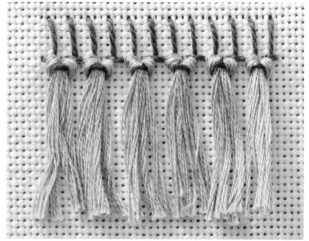

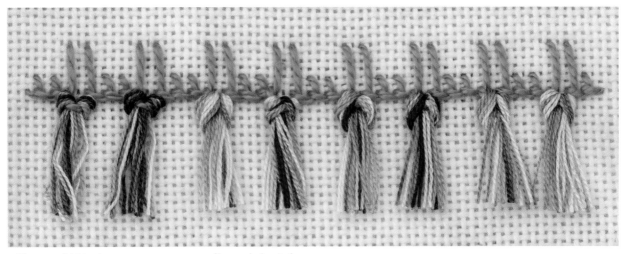

◊ You can add fringing to any arrangement of buttonhole stitch.

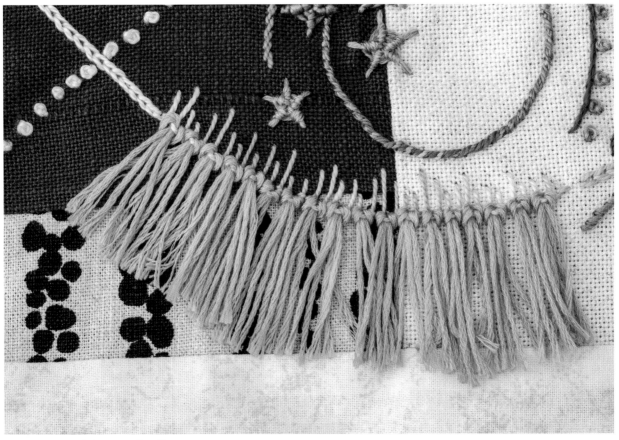

◊ Fringed buttonhole on small wall piece

Buttonhole Stitch (Herring)

Buttonhole herring is a combination of 2 versatile stitches—buttonhole stitch (page 43) and herringbone stitch (page 136). You can change the number and spacing of the buttonhole stitches and the height of the arms. You can also change the height and width of the cross created by the herringbone part of the stitch. Another technique is to use the cross to couch down ribbon or novelty threads. This stitch looks good worked row upon row, back to back, or face to face. You can bead sections of the stitch or arrange the spacing to allow for beads to be added in the gaps created.

1. Buttonhole herring stitch is worked along 3 imaginary horizontal lines. Use the weave of the fabric as your guide, or mark lines on the fabric using a water soluble or fade-out fabric marker.

2. Work a few buttonhole stitches along the top 2 guidelines.

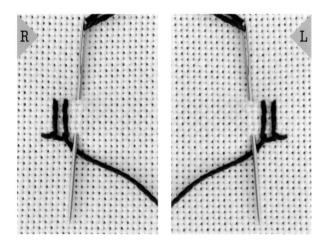

3. Drop to the bottom line and make a small stitch which points to the left (right). Pull the thread through.

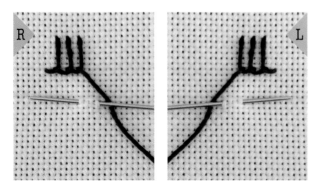

4. Complete the cross by inserting the needle on the same line that is the top of the buttonhole stitches. Have the needle emerge at the base of the buttonhole stitches. Wrap the thread under the needle. Pull the thread through.

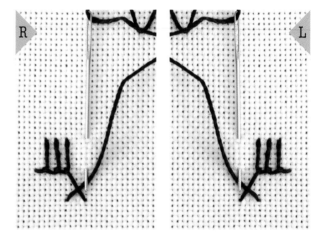

5. Continue the pattern, adding another block of buttonhole stitches before dropping down to add another cross.

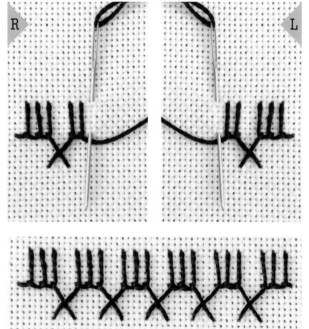

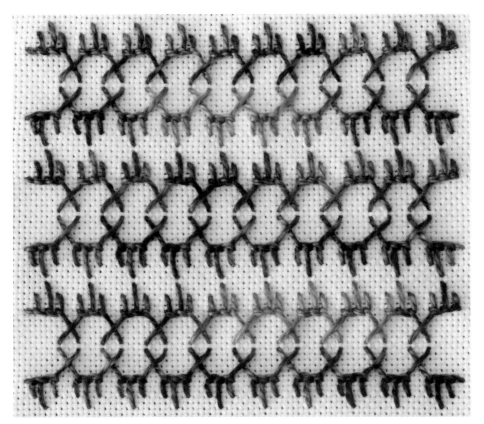

◇ A block of buttonhole herring worked in face-to-face rows

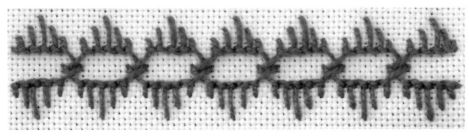

◇ Two rows with the crosses overlapping slightly

§ Back-to-back rows with the buttonhole units worked in triangular shape; and on the lower line,
§ the crosses overlap.

Buttonhole Stitch (Interlaced Up-and-Down)

Interlaced up-and-down buttonhole forms a really attractive band that is ideal to use on a border. It makes a very nice fill too, if you work it row upon row. You can vary the look of this stitch by changing the space between the 2 rows of stitches.

1. Work a line of up-and-down buttonhole stitch (page 67).

2. Turn your work. Bring your needle from the back above the line of stitches and thread the needle under the first bar on the first row. Take care to go under the thread, not through the fabric. Pull the needle through.

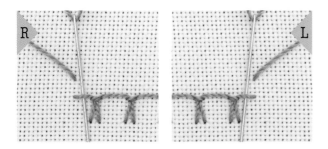

3. Work a pair of up-and-down buttonhole stitches.

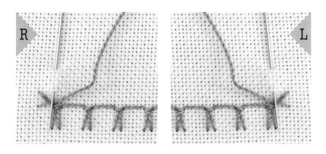

4. Thread your needle under the next bar and take the thread through.

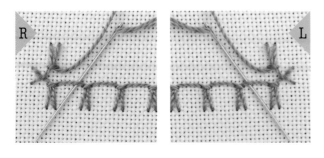

5. Repeat the pattern along the line.

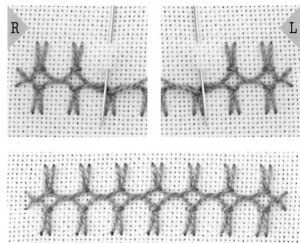

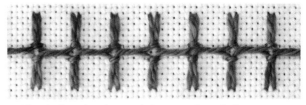

◊ A completed line of interlaced up-and-down buttonhole stitch

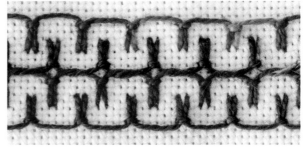

⸕ A band of interlaced up-and-down stitch worked in a variegated hand-dyed perle cotton #8

⸕ This stitch really lends itself to patterning and working in combination with others stitches and beads. This band shows a line of up-and-down buttonhole stitch on either side of interlaced up-and-down buttonhole stitch, all in variegated hand-dyed perle cotton #8.

Buttonhole Stitch (Knotted)

Once you get into a rhythm, knotted buttonhole stitch is quick to work and produces some great twiglike stitches that look like foliage in flower sprays.

1. Make 2 buttonhole stitches (page 43) fairly close together.

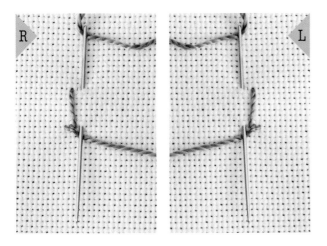

2. Pass the needle under the stitches you just made (not under the fabric). Have your working thread under the needle.

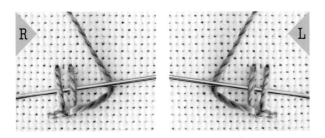

3. Pull the needle through to make a loop. Pull until snug but not too tight.

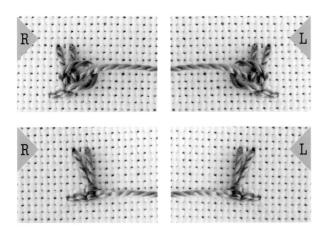

4. Work the next pair of stitches and continue along the line.

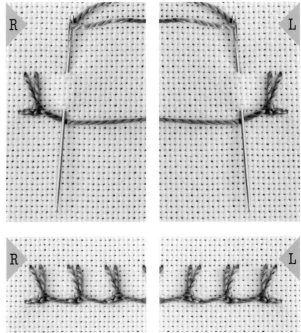

◇ A completed line of knotted buttonhole stitches

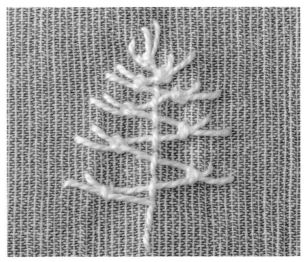

§ Knotted buttonhole worked in a free-form zigzag motion to create a tree shape. Backstitch (page 33) is used for the trunk of the tree.

Buttonhole Stitch (Reversed Bar)

Reversed buttonhole bar creates a textured braidlike stitch that is great to use as a textured border or edging. You can use it as a linear stitch or work it in circles. Since this stitch is worked on a foundation row of buttonhole stitches (page 43), you can use or adapt many of the varieties of buttonhole. This stitch will follow a curve well and you can vary the direction and height of the buttonhole arms to create even more interesting effects.

1. Create a foundation row of buttonhole stitches (page 43) spaced evenly apart. Turn your work so that the base of the buttonhole is at the top.

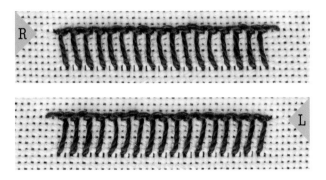

2. Work from right to left (right). Bring your needle out to the right (left) of the first buttonhole ladder. Slide the needle under the bar, then wrap the thread under the needle.

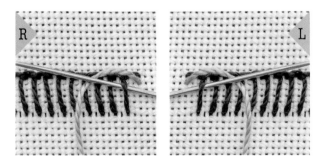

3. Pull the needle through so that the thread forms a loop around the bar. You are not stitching through the fabric, just looping the thread around the bar.

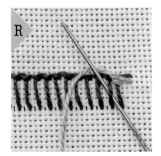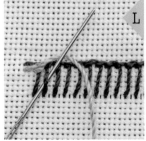

4. Move to the next bar and create a second loop. Continue along the band.

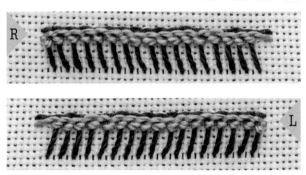

5. You can work as many lines as you wish.

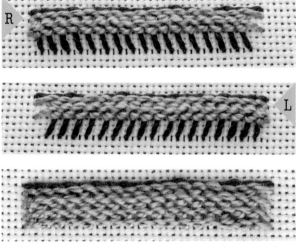

If you totally fill the foundation bars with stitches, you will create a thick braidlike stitch.

Reversed buttonhole bar worked in a circle using a variegated perle cotton #5

Buttonhole Stitch (Threaded Alternating)

With threaded alternating buttonhole, you can develop numerous patterns by simply changing the height of the arms and working row upon row of this stitch. If the rows are offset, you have more options still. You can easily add more interest by using a different thread, even a novelty thread, to lace the stitch.

1. Work a foundation row of alternating buttonhole stitch (page 45).

2. To start threading the stitch, bring up the needle just below the start of the foundation row. Pass your needle under the first set of buttonhole stitches. Pull your thread through. You are lacing the stitch, not passing the needle through the fabric.

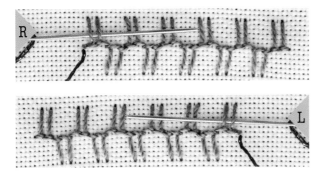

3. Pass the needle under second set of buttonhole stitches. Pull your thread through.

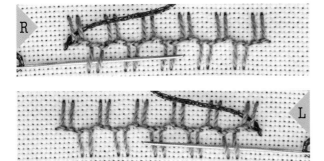

4. Continue this up-and-down motion, lacing your thread along the line.

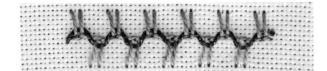

5. When you reach the end of the line, turn your needle and lace the return journey.

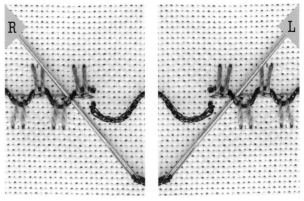

6. When you have laced the line, take your thread to the back of your work. Bring it out to the front a thread or two away to start the return journey of lacing again.

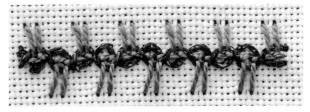

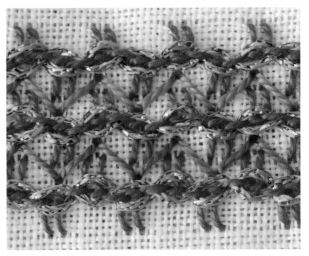

Sample of threaded alternating buttonhole with a row of arrowhead stitch

Buttonhole Stitch (Triangular)

Triangular buttonhole provides a different choice for edgings and for building up patterns. You can add beads at various points in the process, enhancing the stitch in some really nice ways. The shape of the stitch lends itself to stacking row upon row to create patterns, yet, like buttonhole, it can be worked on a gentle curve. You can change the angles to create higher-pointed triangles.

1. This stitch is worked from between 4 imaginary horizontal lines. Start at the base of the lower stitching line and take a 45°-angled stitch to the top line. Bring the needle back out at the original point, with the thread under the needle.

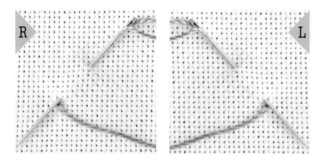

2. Move along the line and make another diagonal stitch, but lower than the first.

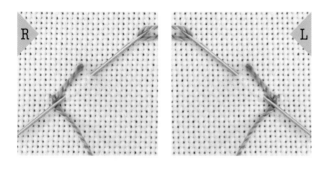

§ Sample of 4 rows worked back to back. You can work rows of this stitch back to back, row upon row, or face to face with the points touching or offset.

3. Move along the line a little and make a third stitch, lower than the first 2.

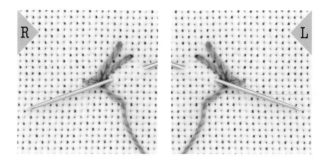

4. Insert the needle at the top of the triangle. Angle the needle so that the tip emerges at the base of the triangle. With the thread under the needle, pull it through the fabric.

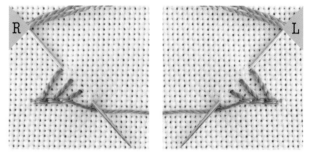

5. Repeat this process along the line.

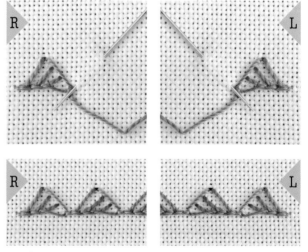

◇ A finished line of triangular buttonhole stitch

Buttonhole Stitch (Up-and-Down)

Up-and-down buttonhole is an incredibly versatile, simple-to-work linear stitch, yet it is a little unusual. You can change the angle and length of the spines to create a variety of looks.

1. Work a single buttonhole stitch (page 43).

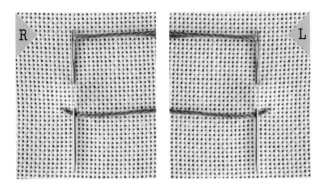

2. Take a bite of the fabric so that the tip of the needle is pointing upward and wrap the working thread under the needle. Pull the needle through, using your opposite thumb to hold down the loop that forms. This is the first pair of tied stitches.

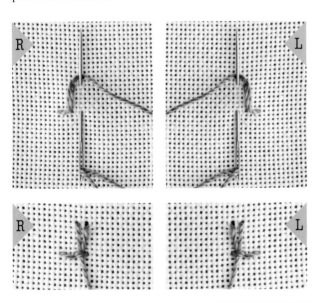

◊ Up-and-down buttonhole worked along a curve, and back to back.

3. Continue along the line. Once you have the rhythm of the stitch, it is easy and quick to do.

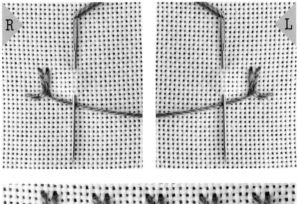

◊ A completed line of up-and-down buttonhole stitch

§ Stacked lines of up-and-down buttonhole, as you would with battlement stitch (page 52).

§ Up-and-down buttonhole worked in a similar manner to double buttonhole stitch (page 57).

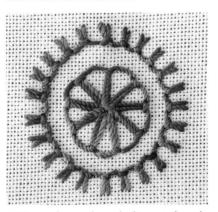

§ The stitch is easily worked in a circle with spines pointing inward or outward.

Buttonhole Stitch (Wheel)

Buttonhole wheel is simply buttonhole stitch worked in a circle. You can vary the center hole by changing the length of the spokes.

1. Mark a circle with a dot in the center. Bring the thread up on the outer line, then insert in the center. Bring the needle up again on the outer line, looping the thread under the needle point.

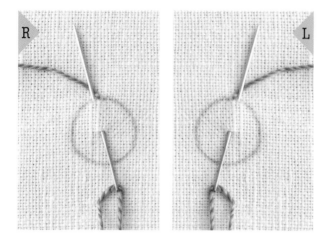

2. Pull the needle through the fabric to form the first spoke of the wheel. Repeat this process around the circle. Try to keep the spokes even.

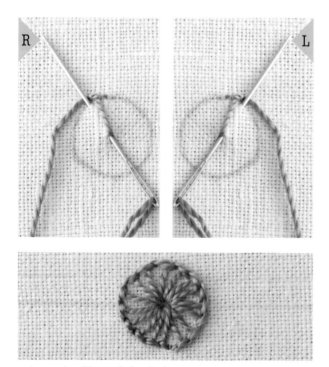

◇ A completed buttonhole wheel

◇ Buttonhole wheels in a contemporary free-form piece

◇ Buttonhole wheels help create a richly textured embroidered surface.

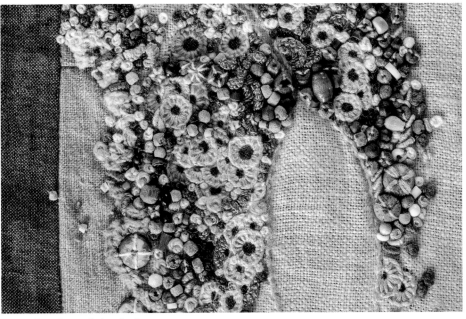

◇ Free-form buttonhole wheels

Tip If you have problems with the rim flicking up and not sitting flat, it means that you are not working enough spokes in the wheel. Add a few more spokes and they will sit flat to the foundation fabric.

Buttonhole Stitch (Wheel Cup)

Buttonhole wheel cups are three-dimensional stitches that make good centers for flowers, such as daffodils.

1. Start by working a buttonhole wheel (page 68). Space the spokes fairly close together but not packed.

2. Bring your thread out on the edge of the wheel. Slide the needle under the first stitch and, with the thread under the needle, pull the thread through. You are working a buttonhole stitch around the edge of the wheel. Do not stitch through the fabric.

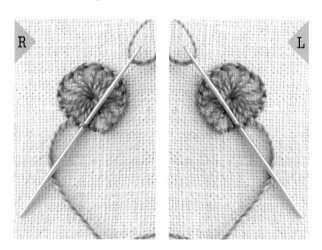

3. Keep going around and around. One row will produce a ridge which you can use.

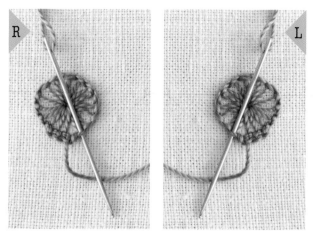

4. Two rows produces a small cup, 3 a deeper cup, and so on. You can stitch beads to the middle of the cup or leave it as a textured stitch.

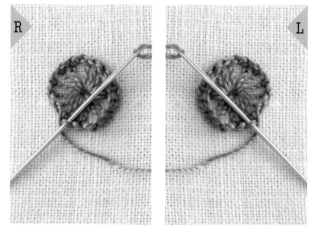

5. To finish, take your thread down the side of the cup.

§ If you want the cup to flare a little, work 2 stitches into the
§ same hole every 2 or 3 stitches.

§ I often tuck buttonhole wheels and buttonhole wheel cups in
§ textured embroidery.

§ Buttonhole wheel cups worked in wool thread are mixed in
§ with beads and textured stitches including buttonhole wheel
§ (page 68), French knots (page 135), bullion knots (page 41),
§ cast-on stitch (page 78), buttonhole bars (page 49), and
§ whipped wheels (page 183).

Buttonhole Stitch (Whipped)

Whipped buttonhole is an easy way to firm up the base-line line of a regular buttonhole stitch, making it an ideal finishing stitch to use on the edge of a project.

If you use a slightly heavier thread in the same color as the foundation stitching, the line you sew will look like a fine cord. For example, if you stitch the foundation stitch in perle cotton #8, use a #5 of the same color to whip it. This is a particularly useful stitch if you need a raised line along an edge.

1. Work a foundation row of buttonhole stitches (page 43).

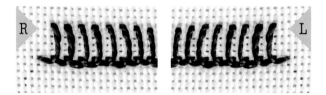

2. Use a blunt-tipped tapestry needle so that you do not split the foundation threads. Bring the needle up at the base of the line of buttonhole stitches. Pass the needle under the base of first buttonhole stitch. Do not pick up any of the fabric. Pull your thread through.

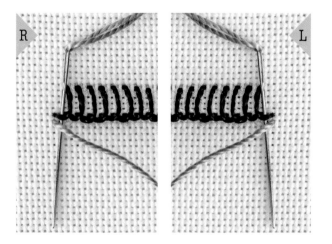

3. Repeat along the length of the row.

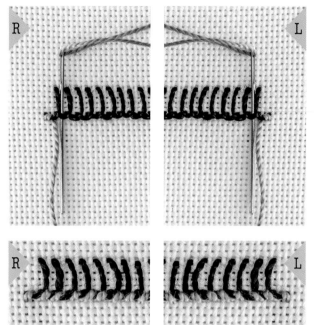

◇ A line of whipped buttonhole stitch

❈ A border band of whipped buttonhole and barb stitch (page 51)

Buttonhole Stitch (Whipped Alternating)

Whipped alternating buttonhole creates a slightly raised fine cordlike line down the central line of alternating buttonhole (page 45). You can use the same thread to whip the line or create a contrast by choosing a different color or textured thread.

1. Work a foundation row of alternating buttonhole stitches (page 45).

2. To whip the row, bring the needle up from the back of the fabric, at the base of the central line. Take the thread over the top of the base of the buttonhole stitches and pass the needle under the first stitch. Do not pick up any of the fabric. Pull the thread through.

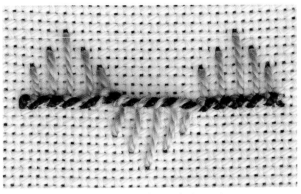

◇ A line of whipped alternating buttonhole stitch

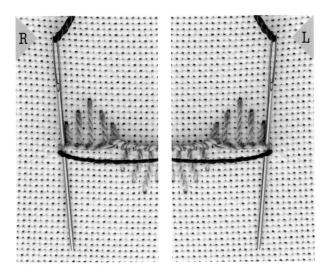

3. Repeat until you have whipped the length of the line.

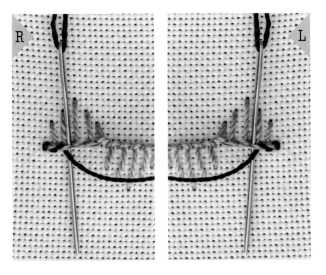

◇ A free-form interpretation of this stitch

Buttonhole Stitch (Zigzag Up-and-Down)

Zigzag up-and-down buttonhole forms a decorative line. If you work it row upon row, it can create a lovely fill with spaces large enough to add another stitch or beads.

1. Work in a zigzag manner along an imaginary horizontal lines. Start with a single set of up-and-down buttonhole stitches (page 67).

2. Insert the needle on the lower line and make an upward stitch with the thread behind the needle.

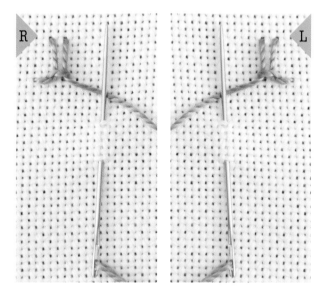

3. Work units of up-and-down buttonhole in a zigzag manner along the line.

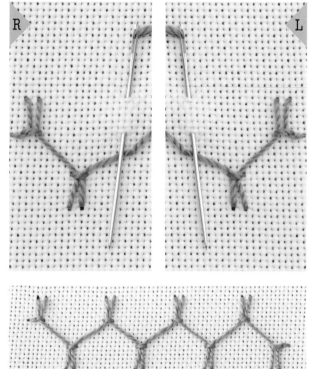

◊ A completed line of zigzag up-and-down buttonhole stitch

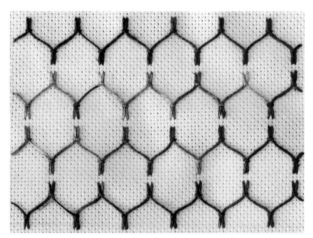

§ Zigzag up-and-down buttonhole stitch worked row upon row to create a fill

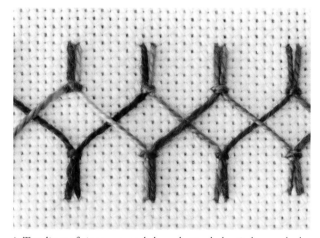

§ Two lines of zigzag up-and-down buttonhole stitches worked offset, with the second row worked on top of the first

Cable Chain Stitch

Cable chain stitch is similar to basic chain stitch (page 80), but with an added step of twisting the thread around the needle after each chain loop. The extra loop between chain stitches creates a link between the chains. Cable chain follows a curve well on both plain and even-weave fabrics.

1. Bring the needle up on the line you want to work. Slip the needle under the thread, then twist the thread around the needle once.

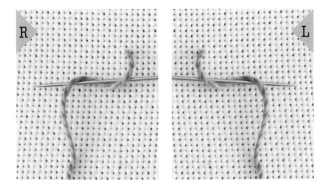

2. Point the needle back into the original hole. Push the thread down the shaft of the needle, so the loop sits close to the fabric. You want a firm but not tight loop around the needle. Bring the needle out below the loop and wrap the thread under the needle point as you would for basic chain stitch.

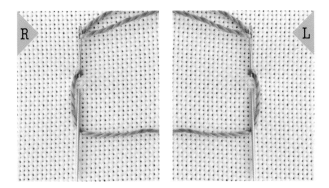

3. Pull the thread through the fabric and you have created your first cable chain stitch.

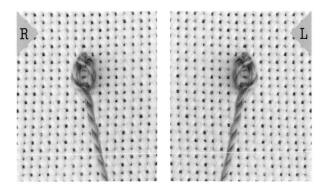

4. Repeat the pattern, creating a knot before moving on to the next chain stitch.

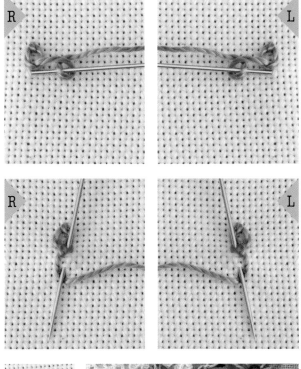

⟡ Line of cable chain stitch ◇ Cable chain stitch in a wall piece

Cable Chain Stitch (Buttonholed)

Cable chain stitch is great combined with a buttonhole stitch, turning it into something quite different from the foundation stitch. This stitch is particularly good when you use a thread with a firm twist such as perle cotton #5 or #8.

In the instructions, I have worked each journey in different colors for clarity, but normally I would work it the same color.

1. Work a row of cable chain stitch (page 75).

2. In the second pass, bring the needle up below the last stitch.. Slip the needle under the thread of the first chain stitch. Loop the thread under the needle point and pull the needle through to make the first buttonhole stitch (page 43).

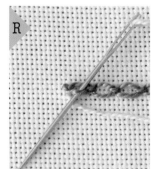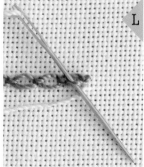

3. Add more buttonhole stitches along the bar until they sit snug. As you work, slide the stitches along the bar so that the finished stitches are spaced closely together. Be careful not to pass the needle through the foundation fabric.

4. When you reach the end of the foundation stitch move to the next chain, skipping the bar between. The bar acts to divide each loop neatly but does not need to be buttonholed.

5. When you reach the end of the row, turn your work and buttonhole the other side of the cable chain foundation.

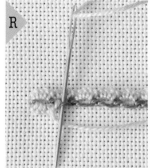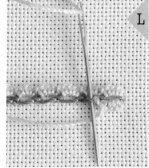

◇ A line of buttonholed cable chain

◇ Buttonholed cable chain stitch used in crazy quilting

Cable Chain Stitch (Knotted)

Knotted cable chain creates an interesting textured line that follows curves well. It is actually a line of oyster stitches (page 87). The second, chain part of the stitch can be lengthened to create quite large loops.

1. Start with an oyster stitch, which will become the first knotted cable chain stitch.

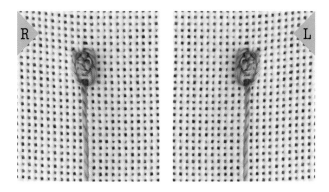

2. Insert your needle a little to the left (right for left-handed) and make a small twisted chain stitch (page 93) just below the oyster stitch.

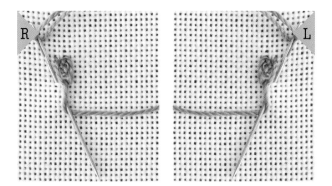

3. Slide the needle under the twist and insert the needle through the fabric behind the top of the twist, and exit below the stitch. Loop the thread under the needle and pull the needle through. Repeat the steps along the column.

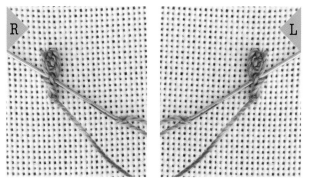

◊ Knotted cable chain creates an interesting line.

◊ Knotted cable chain in a detail of a wall piece

Cast-On Stitch

Cast-on stitch forms little loops that sit proud against the background fabric. This three-dimensional stitch looks outrageously difficult to do, but to be honest, it's not that hard. It is a bit tricky, but fun.

Tips

• Use a milliner's needle.

• Stretch the foundation fabric in an embroidery hoop or frame.

1. Bring the thread to the front of the fabric and take a tiny bite with the needle emerging close to the original hole. Leave the needle in the fabric.

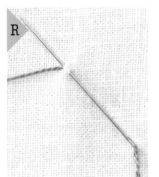 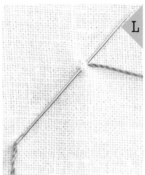

2. You need both hands for this next step, hence the need to have your work mounted in an embroidery hoop. Place the thread over your right (left for left-handed) index finger and rotate your finger, keeping the thread still over your finger but under tension.

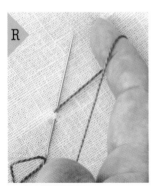 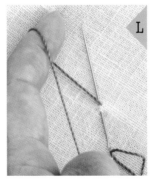

3. This movement of twisting your finger creates a loop around your finger. Transfer the loop from your finger to the needle.

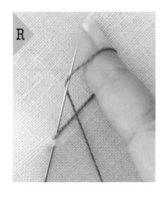 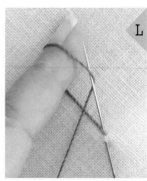

4. Slide the loop down the needle. This action that transfers the loop from finger to needle is similar to casting on a row of stitches on a knitting needle hence the name.

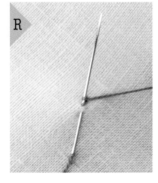 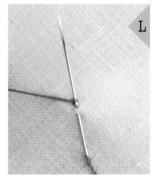

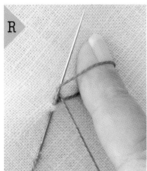 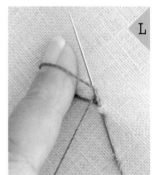

5. Work the required number of cast-on stitches, gently sliding them down the needle as you go. Keep them evenly spaced for best results.

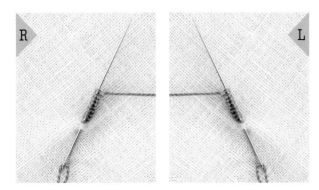

6. Hold the cast-on stitches with the fingers on your left (right) hand and pull the thread with your right (left) hand, through the cast on stitches. Hold the stitches firmly but not so tight you can't pull the needle through.

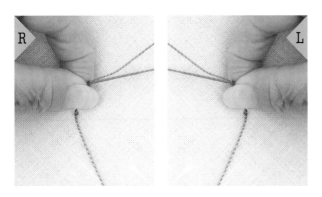

7. Brush the loop into a neat form.

8. Take the needle to the back of the fabric and pull your working thread firmly but not tight to create the loop.

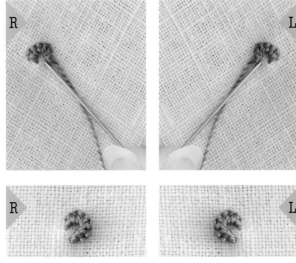

§ The curve of the loop depends upon the number of cast on stitches you use and size of your first backstitch. The higher the number of cast-on stitches, the bigger the loop.

§ Cast-on stitch worked on a crazy quilt block in variegated perle cotton #8

◇ Cast-on stitch worked in variegated perle cotton #8

Chain Stitch

Chain stitch is one of the oldest of the decorative stitches and forms the basis of a large group of stitches. It is tremendously useful as it holds a curve well. A large variety of threads can be used from the finest silk to ribbon.

1. Bring the needle up through the fabric and insert the needle back into the original hole. With the thread wrapped under the needle, pull the needle through the fabric a short distance from the first point.

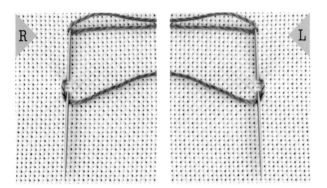

2. Insert the needle into where the thread emerges from the chain. With the thread wrapped under the needle point, pull the needle through the fabric to create the second chain stitch.

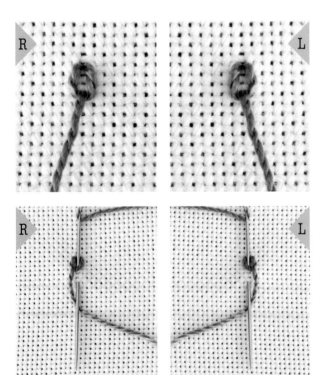

4. Continue the pattern. At the end of the line, tie off with small straight stitch.

◇ A line of chain stitch

◇ Sample of chain stitch in crazy quilting

Chain Stitch (var. Berry Stitch)

Berry stitch is a double detached chain stitch (page 84) that can be worked on any type of fabric. Use a twisted thread such as pearl or soft cotton, ideal because they will help hold the shape.

You can also work this stitch in 2 steps—the first round of chain stitches in one thread weight and the second in a heavier or slightly textured thread.

Or you could work the first round in one color and the second in another. Or substitute the first chain stitch with an oyster stitch (page 87) to produce a textured center.

1. Work a single detached chain stitch (page 84).

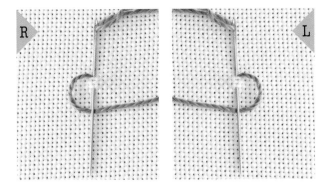

2. Bring the thread out at the top of the chain stitch.

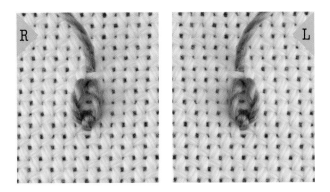

3. Take the needle through the fabric behind the first chain stitch, bringing the point of the needle out a short space below.

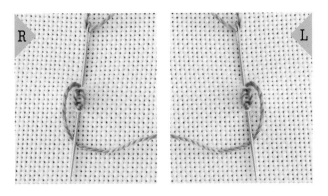

4. With the thread wrapped under the needle point, pull the needle through the fabric to make the second chain stitch. Make a small straight stitch to secure the second chain stitch.

◇ A sample of berry stitch

◇ Berry stitch worked in variegated perle cotton #5

Chain Stitch (Butterfly)

Butterfly chain stitch is versatile and decorative. If you vary threads and the angle of the stitches, you can create a lot of interesting effects. Butterfly chain stitch easily follows a curve, so you can develop a totally different look to the stitch simply by letting it follow a gentle line.

Take advantage of contrasting threads. Since butterfly chain stitch is worked in 2 journeys, it is easy to change color or type of thread.

1. Work a foundation of groups of 3 straight stitches.

2. On the second journey, bring the needle out above the stitches. Pass the needle under the 3 straight stitches (not through the fabric), and wrap the thread across and under the needle. Pull the needle through to clutch the group of 3 stitches together; this forms a twisted chain stitch (page 93).

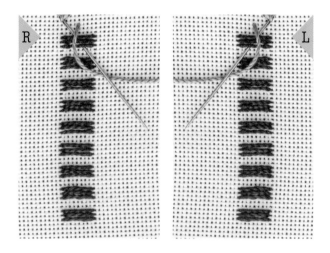

3. Continue in this manner along the line. Do not allow the needle to enter the ground fabric except at the beginning and end of the row.

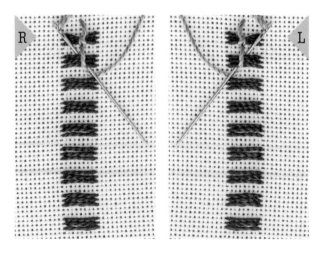

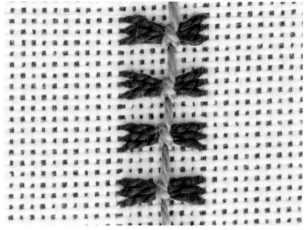

◊ A line of butterfly chain

◊ The thread that you use to clutch the foundation stitches together can be of heavier weight or a different color. It is traditional to work a foundation row of 3 vertical straight stitches, but you can vary their length.

◊ In this sample, the groups have been worked in zigzag manner.

◊ You can also arrange the foundation blocks of stitches in squares.

Chain Stitch (Chained Bar)

Chained bar stitch forms a solid line that is ideal for borders, or you can use it to couch down ribbons, novelty yarns, tape, or flat braids.

1. Lay down some long straight stitches. Between 2 and 6 straight stitches in DMC perle cotton #3 works well.

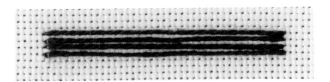

2. Work a zigzag chain stitch (page 99) across the bar.

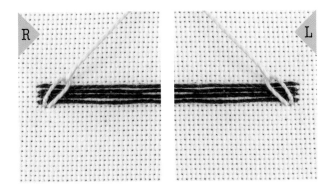

3. In the second stitch, turn the angle of the chain stitch to take the chain over the bar.

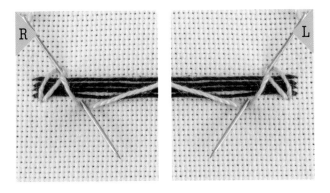

4. Continue along the bar until the straight stitches are couched down by the zigzag chain stitches.

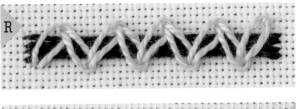

◇ A line of chained bar

◇ Lines of chained bar stitch in variegated thread

Chain Stitch (Detached) (*also* Lazy Daisy Stitch)

Detached chain, also known as *lazy daisy stitch*, is often one of the first that people learn in order to create flowers and petals, but it is not the only way you can use this stitch. It is called detached chain stitch because that is what it is—a single chain stitch (page 80).

1. Bring the needle up through the fabric. Insert the needle so that the point emerges a short space away.

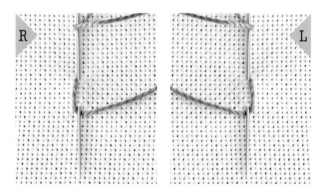

2. With the thread wrapped under the needle point pull the needle through the fabric.

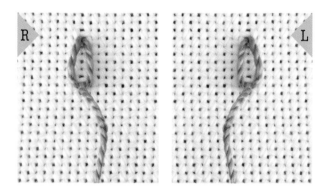

3. Take the needle to the back of the fabric by making a small straight stitch. This will secure and complete the stitch.

◇ A detached chain stitch

◊ A small floral motif worked in detached chain stitch, stem stitch (page 167), and French knots (page 135)

◊ A small floral motif worked in detached chain stitch, feather stitch (page 124), and French knots (page 135)

Tip

Here is an easy way to work stitches in a circle. This works for detached chain stitch flowers, oyster stitch (page 87), bullion knot (page 41) flowers, whipped long-tail chain stitch (page 96), and stitches where you have to work a circle of spokes that radiate from the center:

1. Imagine a clock face. Work a stitch at 12 o'clock, another stitch at 6 o'clock, at 3 o'clock, and at 9 o'clock.

2. Add a stitch between 12 and 3 o'clock and another between 3 and 6 o'clock and so on.

If you do this, you will have a nicely balanced hand-embroidered flower without having to mark the fabric.

Chain Stitch (Feathered)

Feathered chain is a long-tail chain stitch (page 86) worked in a zigzag manner.

1. Make the first step of a chain stitch (page 80), on the diagonal.

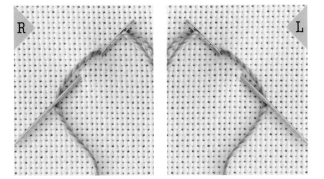

2. Tie the chain down with a long straight stitch on the diagonal.

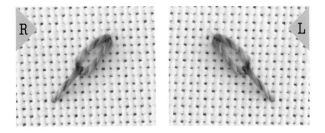

3. Bring the needle up through the fabric, close to the end of the tie stitch. Have 1 or 2 threads between where the tie stitch went into the fabric and where your needle emerges.

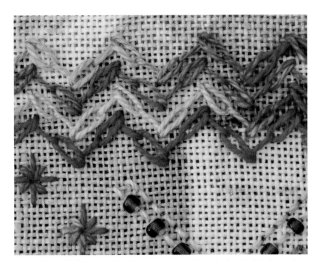

◊ Feathered chain worked in variegated hand-dyed silk thread that is the same thickness as perle cotton #8

4. Work another chain stitch pointing back toward the upper imaginary line.

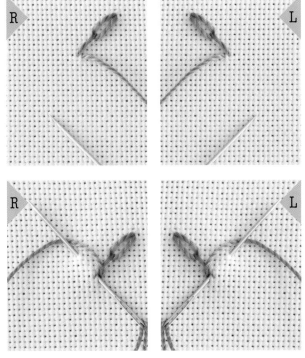

5. Tie the stitch off with a long straight stitch.

6. Continue each stitch on the diagonal to create a zigzag.

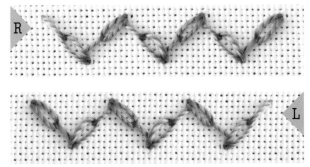

◊ A line of feathered chain

Chain Stitch (Long-Tail)

Long-tail chain is simply a chain stitch (page 80) secured with a long tie stitch. The stitch is not difficult to work and is delightful to use as a quick, light fill to sprinkle across an area in a free-form manner. You can also take advantage of the straight stitch that secures the chain, and weave or whip the spokes as in whipped long-tail chain stitch (page 96).

1. Bring the needle up through the fabric. Insert it back where it emerged, and take a small bite of the fabric, wrapping the thread under the needle.

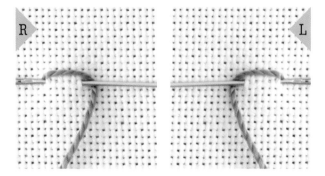

2. Pull the needle through to create a chain stitch. On the same line, tie the chain down with a long straight stitch.

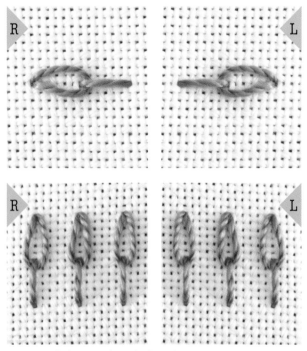

◇ Long-tail chain stitch worked in a line

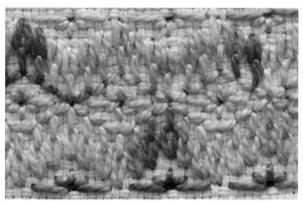

◇ Long-tail chain stitch worked in a waved line

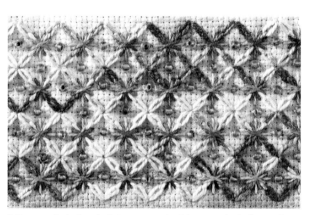

◇ Long-tail chain stitch interspaced with crossed stitches and beads on hand-painted Aida cloth

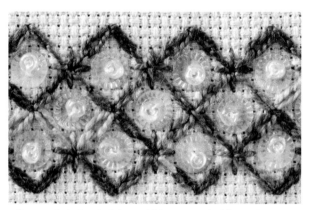

◇ Long-tail chain stitch in a grid interspaced with sequins

Chain Stitch (var. Oyster Stitch)

Oyster stitch is actually a single knotted cable chain stitch. You can often use oyster stitch in situations where you would use a detached chain stitch (page 84). It creates a textured, slightly raised stitch that adds variety. If you work this stitch in a line, it becomes knotted cable chain stitch (page 77).

1. Start with a twisted chain stitch (page 93).

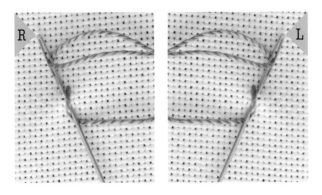

2. Pull the working thread snug, until the stitch lies flat, but not so tight that it pulls on the fabric. Pass the needle under the right-hand (left-hand) top thread above the loop. Slide the needle through without picking up the foundation fabric.

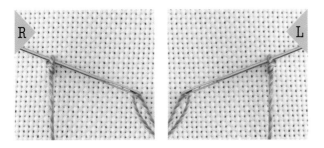

3. Insert the needle through the fabric at the top of the stitch, and behind the knot and exit below the stitch.

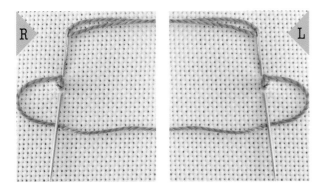

4. Loop the thread under the needle and pull the needle through. Tie off with a small straight stitch as you would for chain stitch.

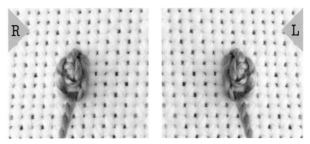

◊ Oyster stitch

Oyster stitch is most often used as buds in floral motifs or worked in a circle with the stitches pointing outward to create flowers. This sample was worked using a variegated perle cotton #5.

Chain Stitch (Threaded)

This stitch follows a curve well, and you can add lots of variety by using interesting threads or adding beads.

1. Work a row of chain stitch (page 80). Using a blunt-ended tapestry needle, so that the foundation threads do not split, start to weave a second thread under each of the chain stitches. Slide the needle under the first chain stitch.

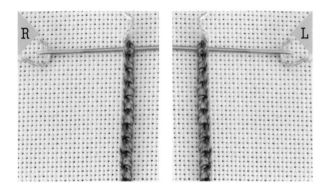

2. Turn the needle and slide it under the second chain stitch, leaving a small loop at the side.

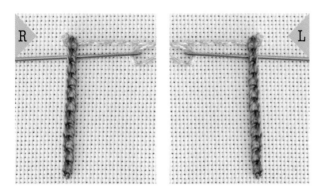

3. Weave the length of the row and take the thread to the back of the fabric.

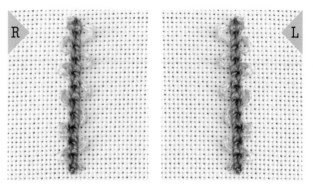

◇ A line of threaded chain

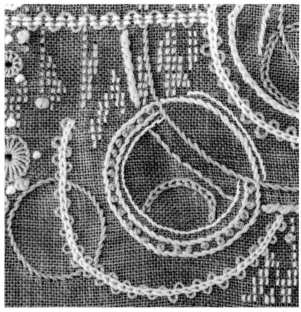

§ A detail from a free-form sampler of linear stitches including threaded chain stitch.

Chain Stitch (Triple)

Triple chain is quite quick and easy to work, as it is a chain stitch with 2 side stitches. This can be very effective, particularly if you vary the height or angle of the chain stitches down the side.

1. Start with a chain stitch (page 80).

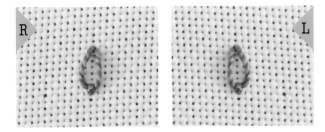

2. Form a second chain stitch on the left (right for left-handed), at a right angle to the first. Make sure the chain stitch tie is pointed to the middle of the line.

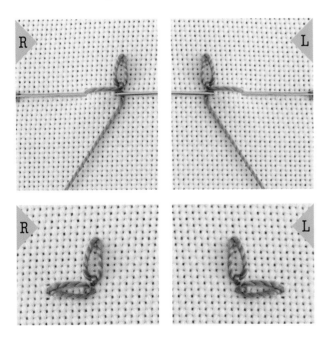

3. Work another chain stitch on the other side of the central line. The tie stitch of all 3 chain stitches should point to the middle.

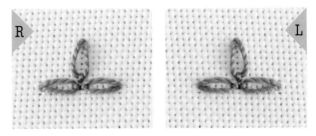

4. Bring the thread out in the middle of the center chain stitch.

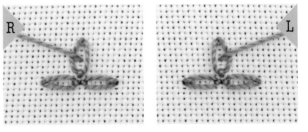

5. Insert the needle at the point where the thread emerged and make a vertical chain. Pull the thread through at the left (right for left-handed).

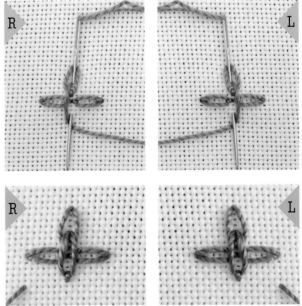

6. Make the 2 chain stitches to form a second wing.

Repeat the process along the line.

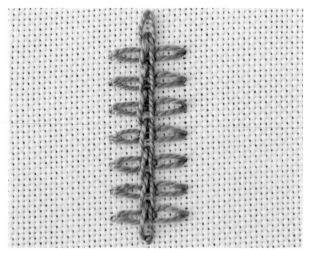

◇ Triple chain stitch

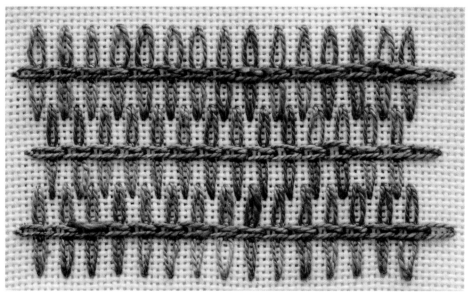

⧝ Triple chain stitch worked horizontally, row upon row, in a hand-dyed variegated silk thread
⧝ the same thickness as perle cotton #8

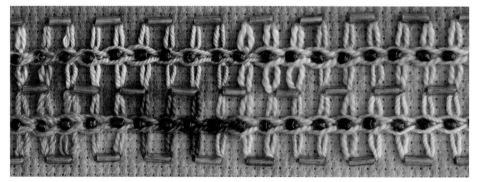

⧝ Triple chain stitch worked on hand painted Aida cloth using a variegated perle cotton #5.
⧝ Beads were added last.

Chain Stitch (var. Tulip Stitch)

Tulip stitch is also known as slipped detached chain stitch. This simple stitch can look like a small tulip—hence the name. You can work the chain part of the stitch in 1 thread and change threads for the slipped straight stitches. The height of the detached chain can be varied, as well as the angle of the straight stitches. It is effective worked in perle threads, wool, ribbon, and fine metallic cords.

1. Make a single detached chain stitch (page 84).

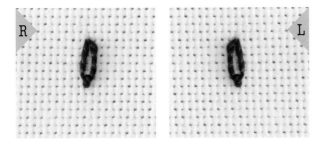

2. Bring the needle up on one side of the detached chain. Slide the needle under the tie of the detached chain.

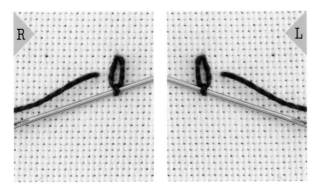

3. Take the thread through and insert your needle on the other side of the detached chain to create a curve.

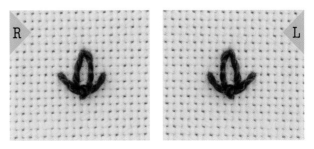

4. You can have 1, 2, or more of these base stitches at varying angles.

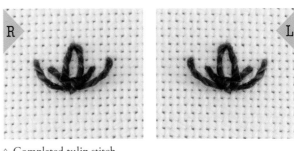

◊ Completed tulip stitch

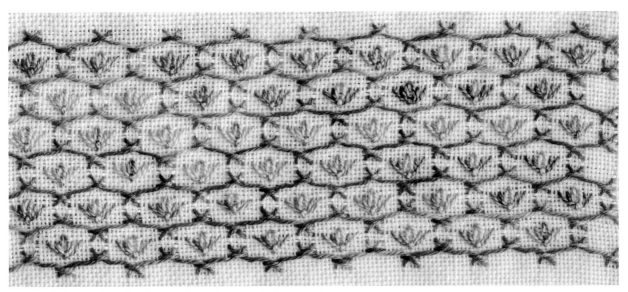

◊ Lines of tulip stitch worked between lines of tied herringbone stitch (page 145)

◇ Tulip stitch worked with 3 slipped stitches at the base

⸙ Tulip stitch worked using an oyster stitch (page 87) instead of a chain stitch and with 3 slipped ⸙ stitches at the base.

⸙ Tulip stitch worked using an oyster stitch (page 87) instead
⸙ of a chain stitch, and with 4 slipped stitches at the base, each
⸙ worked in a different thread

◇ Tulip stitch worked in a square

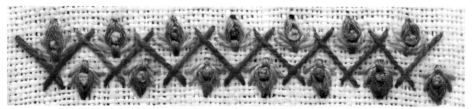

⸙ A line of tulip stitch worked in the V of the herringbone stitch (page 136). I added a French knot
⸙ (page 135) to the middle of each chain stitch.

Chain Stitch (Twisted)

Twisted chain stitch easily follows curves and works well on all types of fabrics. This stitch is suitable for free-form stitching and easily combines with beads. The size and appearance of the stitch will be influenced by the size and spacing of the prongs.

Twisted chain stitch is great for producing a textured line. You can experiment with different threads and it combines well with other textured stitches. You can overlap lines of the stitch or use it to couch down another thread.

1. Start with a basic chain stitch (page 80).

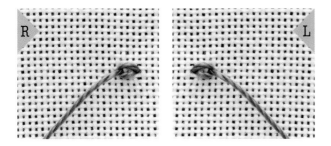

2. Insert the needle above the first stitch. This can vary depending upon how wide you want the "spike" of the chain. The wider the gap, the larger the spike that is formed. Have the point of the needle emerge a short space along the line. Wrap the thread under the needle.

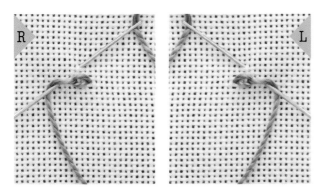

3. Pull the needle through the fabric. The thread should cross as you do this, producing a crossed chain stitch.

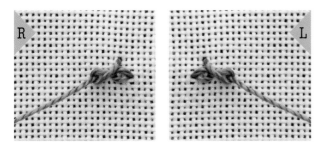

4. Continue down the line.

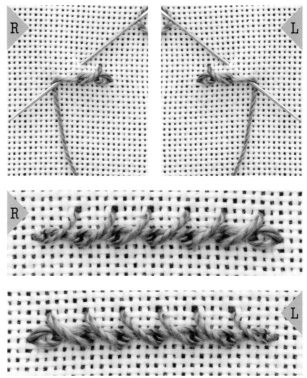

◇ A line of twisted chain stitch

§ Free-form twisted chain stitch worked in perle cotton #5, linen thread, silk thread, and stranded cotton floss combined with beads

Chain Stitch (Whipped 1)

Whipped chain stitch creates a slightly stronger line than ordinary chain stitch. It stands a little more proudly off the surface. This is a particularly useful stitch if a raised line is required on a delicate, fine fabric that will not take a heavy thread through the weave. You can work a foundation row of stitches in a fine thread, then whip the line with a heavier thread.

The thread with which you whip the foundation line of chain stitches can be a contrasting color or texture. You can use many novelty threads with this technique.

1. Work a foundation row of chain stitch (page 80). Make each chain stitch slightly longer and a little looser than normal, because the line of stitching will tighten slightly when you whip it, and you don't want your work to pucker.

2. With a second thread, whip the foundation row by passing the needle under each chain stitch.

Tip To avoid splitting the foundation stitches, try passing the needle eye first. This is an alternative to switching to a blunt-tipped tapestry needle for the whipping process.

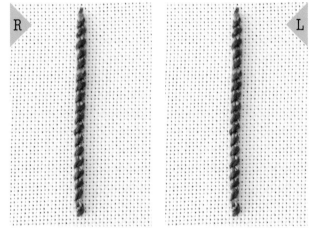

◇ A completed line of whipped chain stitches

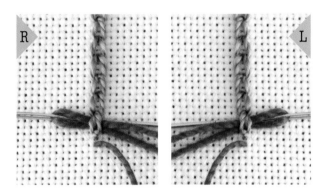

3. Continue whipping the line of stitches. Take care not to stitch through the fabric.

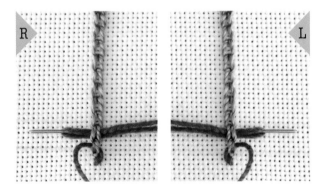

§ Free-form sampler of linear stitches including whipped chain
§ stitch 1

Chain Stitch (Whipped 2)

This is a fun version of whipped chain. Instead of whipping over each chain stitch, as you do in version 1, you whip both sides of the chain, working up the first side of the line then back down the other. It produces a stitch that looks totally different and is particularly effective if you use a contrasting thread or a metallic thread.

1. Work a foundation row of chain stitch.

2. Use a blunt-ended tapestry needle to avoid splitting the chain stitches on the foundation row. Bring your needle out at the start of the line and pass it under one side of the first chain stitch. Pull your needle through. Take care not to pick up any of the fabric.

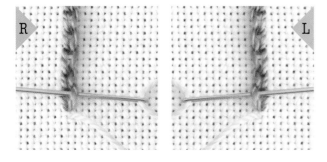

3. Continue whipping the side of each chain stitch down the line. Take your thread to the back of the work and tie off.

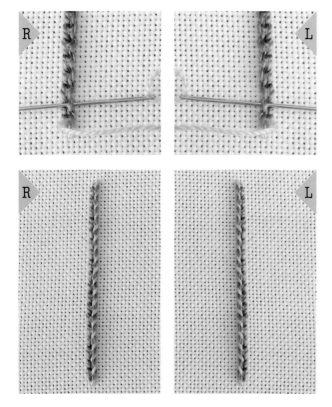

4. Bring the needle out at the start of the line and repeat the same whipping action along the other side of the foundation chain stitches.

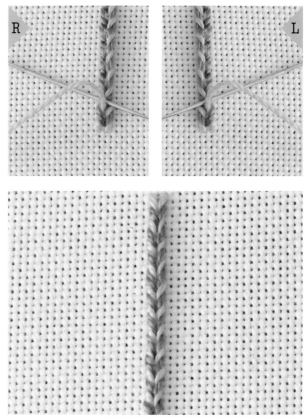

◇ Whipped chain stitch 2

⸘ A detail from a free-form sampler of linear stitches, including
⸘ whipped chain stitch 2

Chain Stitch (Whipped Long-Tail)

With this stitch, you can create interesting flowers, fills, and accents.

1. Work 8 long-tail chain stitches (page 86) so that they radiate in a circle. The tails of the stitch are the foundation threads for the whipped stitches.

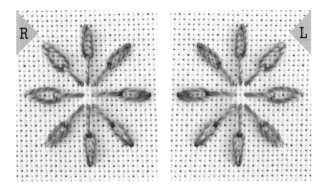

2. Bring the thread out near center and slide the needle under 2 tails and pull the thread through. Take care not to stitch through the fabric.

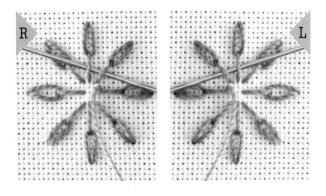

3. In this stitch, you are not going through the fabric but making a series of backstitches over the tails. Slide the needle under the first two long tails. Pull the needle through. Move back one tail and slide the needle under two tails. Pull the needle through. This whipping action of under two tails and back one tail creates the stitch.

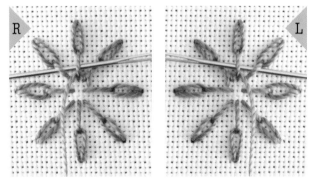

4. Repeat, whipping each tail as you progress around the wheel until the circle is filled.

◇ Whipped long-tail chain

◇ Sample on a free-form improvisational piece

Chain Stitch (Whipped Triple)

With whipped triple chain stitch, you can add wonderful variety to your embroidery. It looks complex yet is deceptively simple.

1. Work a foundation line of triple chain stitch (page 89).

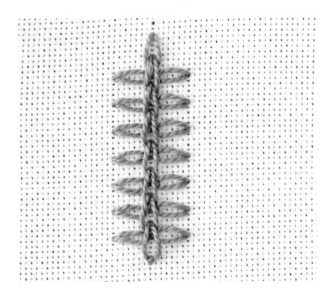

2. Use a blunt-ended tapestry needle to avoid splitting the stitches on the foundation row. Whip the central line of chain stitches. The technique is the same as whipped chain stitch 2 (page 95). Bring your needle out at the start of the line and pass it under one side of the first stitch. With your needle pointed toward the center line, pull your needle through.

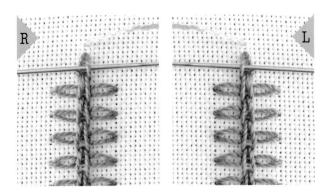

3. Continue whipping down one side of the triple chain stitch. Take your thread to the back of the work and tie it off.

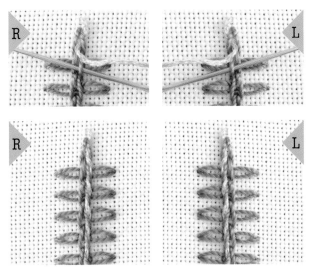

4. Repeat the same whipping action along the other side of the central chain stitches. With each stitch, make sure your needle is pointed toward the center line and take care not to pick up any of the fabric.

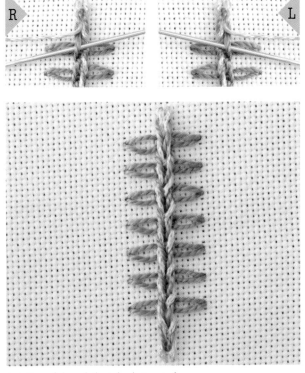

◇ A line of threaded triple chain stitch

Chain Stitch (Woven Detached)

Woven detached chain stitch creates delightful little leaf shapes that can be used in floral sprays. It consists of a detached chain stitch (page 84) that has been woven with a secondary thread. It looks effective if you use a variegated thread to weave the stitch.

1. Work a detached chain stitch in slightly loose manner, since the loop of the chain stitch acts as the foundation on which to weave. The weaving will pull the thread tighter.

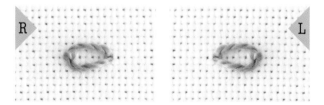

2. Take a thread to the back and bring it out at the top of the chain stitch. Slide your needle under one side of the chain stitch, pointing the needle toward the center. Do not go through the fabric, just under the loop of the chain stitch. Pull the needle through.

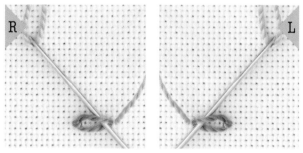

◊ I used 2 thread colors so you can see the weaving action.

3. Slide the needle under the loop of the chain stitch, keeping the needle pointing toward the center. Pull the needle through.

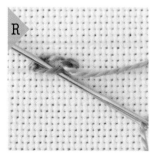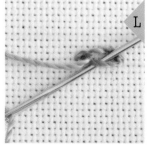

4. Repeat this weaving action back and forth. As you weave, pack the weaving slightly by nudging the weaving up the chain stitch with the end of the needle.

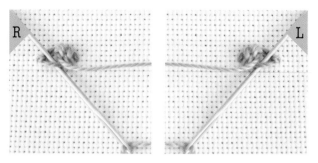

5. When you get to the base of the chain stitch, take your thread to the back of your work and finish off. As you can see, the stitch makes a little leaf shape.

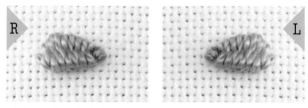

◊ Woven detached chain

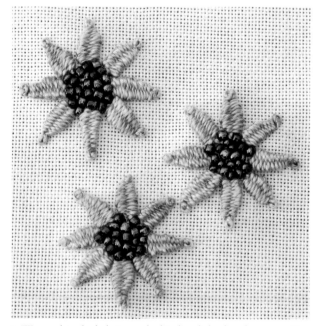

◊ Woven detached chain worked in hand-dyed perle cotton #5

Chain Stitch (Zigzag)

Zigzag chain stitch is effective when worked alone. You also can stack it row upon row to build up patterns to be used as a fill or for borders.

1. Make a chain stitch (page 80) at an upward diagonal.

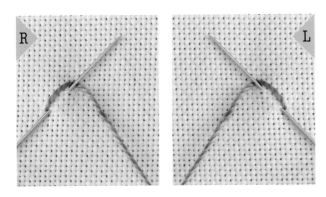

2. Bring the needle back up at the top of the previous stitch and make a second chain stitch at a downward angle.

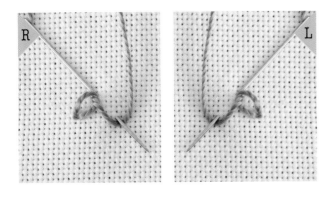

3. Continue along the line, working each loop at right angles to the previous loop to create the zigzag line.

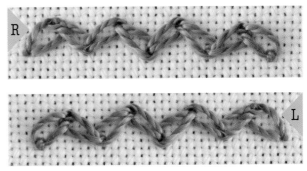

◊ Zigzag chain stitch

Tip If your loops flip up as you enter the fabric with each loop, pierce the end of the previous loop. This will ensure that each section of the chain lies flat.

◊ Detached chain stitches arranged in a zigzag pattern

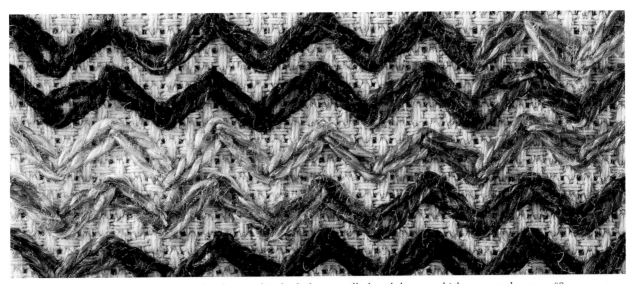

◊ Lines of zigzag chain stitch, worked on hand-painted Aida cloth using silk thread the same thickness as perle cotton #8

Chevron Stitch

Chevron stitch is a tremendously versatile decorative stitch. You can change the spacing of the feet, or the height and width of the stitch to create different patterns.

1. Work from left to right (right to left for left-handed) on 2 imaginary horizontal lines. Bring the thread out on the top line. Move a little to the right (left) on the same line and take a stitch with the needle emerging in the middle under the stitch.

2. Take the needle diagonally and insert it on the lower line, Make a small stitch to the left (right), about the same size as the small stitch on the first line.

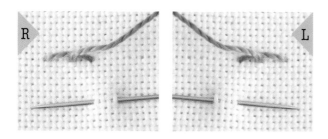

3. Pull the needle through, On the same line, take a longer stitch that forms the foot, bringing the needle back up at the base of the diagonal stitch.

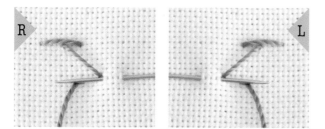

4. Take your needle to the top line and repeat the process. Continue the pattern down the line.

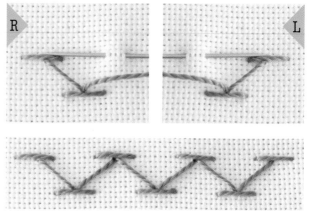

◇ Chevron stitch

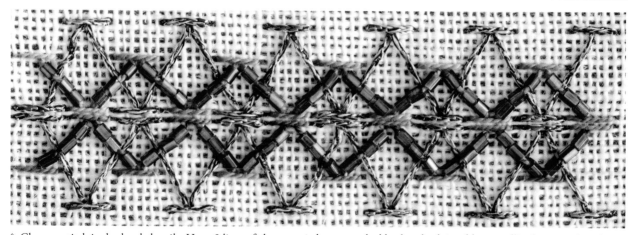

§ Chevron stitch is also beaded easily. Here, 2 lines of chevron stitch were worked back to back in a blue metallic chainette thread.
§ The next journey, I stacked 2 lines of beaded chevron stitch worked back to back.

Chevron Stitch (Double)

Double chevron stitch is a very simple variety of chevron stitch (previous page), since it is worked in 2 journeys that can be used to great effect. The samples have been worked in 2 thread colors so that the second journey can be seen more easily. You can work double chevron in a single color or switch the threads to create interesting patterns.

1. Work a row of chevron stitch (previous page) from left to right between 2 imaginary horizontal lines. Space the stitches evenly.

2. Work a second row of chevron stitch in the spaces between the first.

⧓ Double chevron stitch worked row upon row, back to back, with the second row beaded

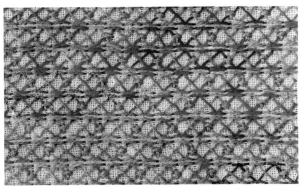

⧓ Double chevron worked in perle cotton #5, metallic, and silk threads. Every second cross bar is tied with a cross-stitch.

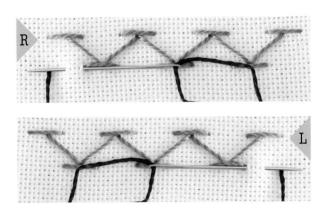

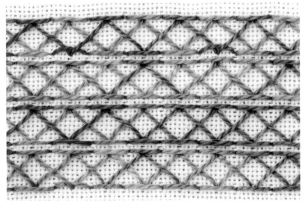

⧓ Double chevron can easily become a quickly worked filling. Here it is worked in Caron Watercolour perle cotton #5.

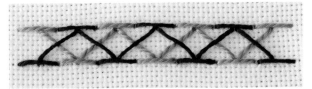

◇ A line of double chevron stitch

Chevron Stitch (Fringed)

You can add a fringe to many stitches. All you need is a loop somewhere in the formation of the stitch from which to hang them. Or in the case of chevron stitch, you can fringe the base line of the stitch.

1. Work a line of chevron stitch (page 100).

2. Cut 2 or 3 threads into lengths of about 2″–4″ (5–10 cm) and lay them together. Fold them in half. With a crochet hook, pick up the threads at the halfway point and hook them under the stitch to form a loop.

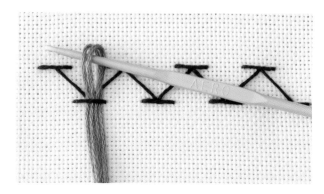

3. Fold the loop over the foundation stitch and pull the tail through the loop.

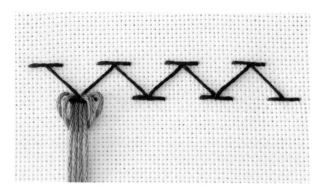

4. Pull the tail gently until the loop sits neatly on the foundation stitch. Continue along the line. Trim the fringe last, as that way you will get it straight.

◊ Fringed chevron stitch

Tip If you want to experiment with fringing other stitches, the main criteria to look for is a stitch that has a base line that forms a solid line. Stitches such as buttonhole stitch (page 43), buttonhole wheel (page 68), half-chevron stitch (page 103), and backstitch (page 33) work well.

Chevron Stitch (Half-Chevron)

Half-chevron stitch follows curves well and can create a useful border or outline stitch. You can easily create patterns with this stitch as it looks good worked back to back, face to face, and offset. You can change the height and spacing of this stitch to create numerous varieties.

1. Work from left to right (right to left for left-handed) on 2 imaginary horizontal lines. If needed, mark guidelines on the fabric using a fade-out or water-dissolvable pen. Bring the thread out on the left end, between the top and bottom line. Insert the needle a little to the right (left) on the top line and take a small straight downward stitch with the thread looped under the needle. This is like making half a Cretan stitch (page 111).

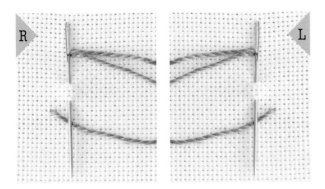

2. Pull the needle through. Insert your needle on the lower imaginary line and make a small stitch. This part of the stitch is like making half a chevron stitch (page 100).

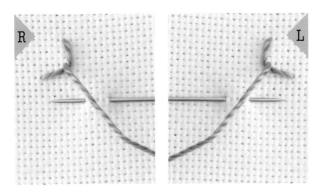

3. Move the needle to the right (left) as you would with chevron stitch and take a bite of the fabric to make the foot of the stitch.

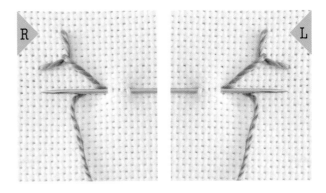

4. Move to the upper right (left) and make a small downward stitch.

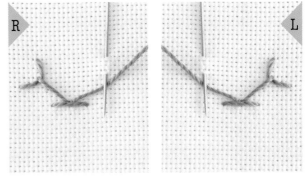

5. Repeat the pattern along the row.

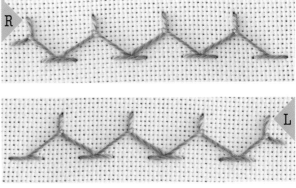

◇ Half-chevron stitch

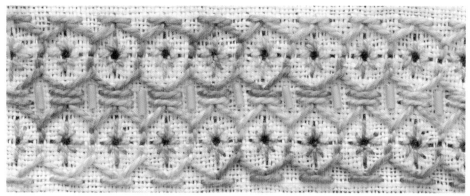

◊ Rows of half-chevron stitch worked face to face with Algerian eye stitch (page 28) worked in the spaces

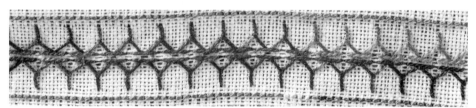

◊ Half-chevron stitch is very effective worked back to back and you can build up interesting and complex patterns using it.

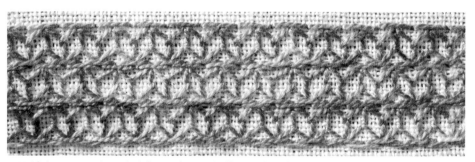

◊ Half-chevron stitch worked face to face and offset, with each row tucked into the other.

◊ Two rows of half-chevron stitch worked back to back with beads stitched into the spaces

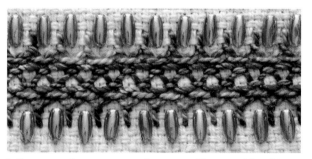

◊ You can easily create a complex pattern if you combine this stitch with others. Here, a row of half-chevron stitch is combined with stepped and threaded running stitch 1 (page 157) followed by half-chevron stitch. Beads were added in the spaces.

Chevron Stitch (Herringbone)

Chevron herringbone is made up of one part chevron stitch (page 100) and one part herringbone stitch (page 136). It can be used as a border or may be built up row upon row to create embellished textures. You can change the height and spacing to create numerous varieties.

1. Work from left to right (right to left for left-handed) on 2 imaginary lines. Bring the thread from the back of the fabric on the bottom line. Move diagonally to the top line. Take a bite of the fabric to the left (right) and pull the needle through to make the first diagonal stitch. Take the needle diagonally down to the bottom line and insert it with the tip pointing left (right). Pull the needle through.

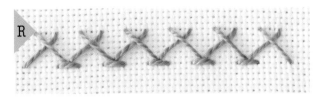

◊ Chevron herringbone stitch

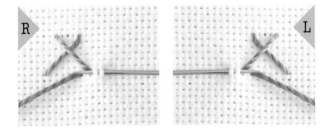

§ Two lines of chevron herringbone stitch worked face to face, with a seed bead stitched down the center line.

2. Make a small foot bar stitch, as you would a chevron stitch, by moving to the right (left), inserting the needle to have tip emerging at the base of the diagonal stitch. Pull the thread through.

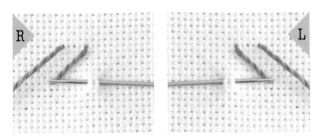

§ Two lines of chevron herringbone stitch worked back to back with a seed bead stitched down the center line

§ Two lines are worked face to face in perle cotton #5 and placed so they tuck in to each other.

3. Take your needle to the top line and repeat the process. Continue the pattern down the row.

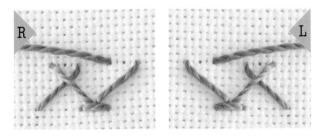

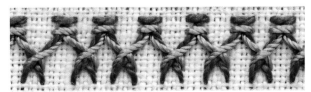

§ Two rows, with the second row worked on top of the first using a different thread.

Chevron Stitch (Squared)

Squared chevron stitch can be used as a single unit or worked in lines to build up patterns. Its geometric shape lends itself to beautiful patterning.

Think in terms of defining the corners of each square with the foot of a chevron stitch.

1. Bring your needle up at what would be the left (right) corner of the square. Move up diagonally to take a stitch at the top corner of the square.

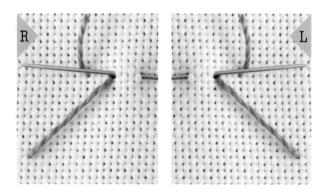

2. Take another stitch that comes out at the top corner.

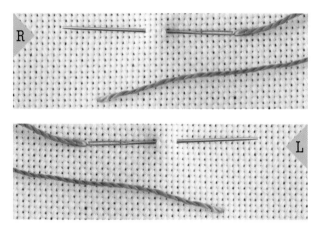

3. Take the needle diagonally to the right (left) corner and make an upward stitch.

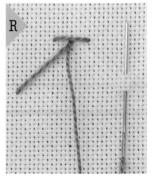
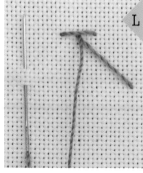

4. Take another stitch that comes out at the right (left) corner.

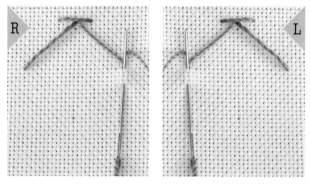

5. Continue to form the bottom corner and left (right) corner.

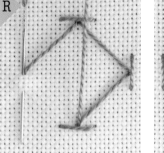
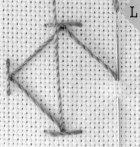
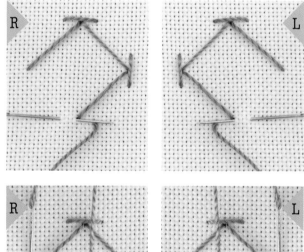

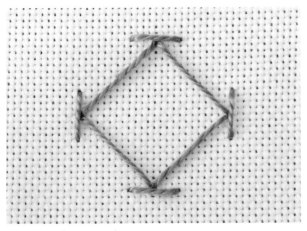

◊ Squared chevron stitch

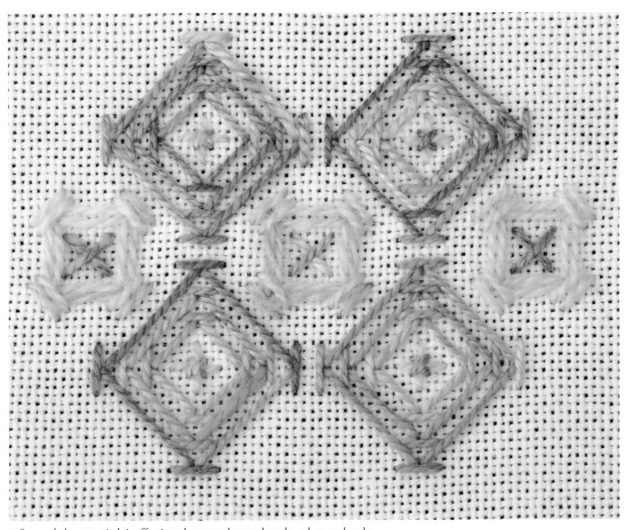

◊ Squared chevron stitch is effective when you change threads, colors, and scale.

Chevron Stitch (Stepped)

Stepped chevron is simply a double chevron stitch (page 101), where the second journey is larger than the first. To change the patterns created with this stitch, experiment with the spacing of both journeys and the height of both journeys. There is also the opportunity to explore using different threads.

This stitch is a decorative way to hold down a ribbon or couch down thicker threads.

1. Work a row of chevron stitch (page 100) with each stitch a little apart, so you have room for the second row. Bring the second thread below the first row.

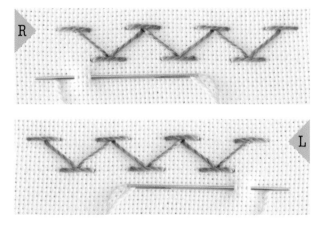

◊ A line of stepped chevron stitch

2. Work a taller line of chevron stitch, placing each stitch between the V's of the first line.

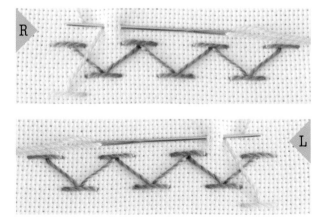

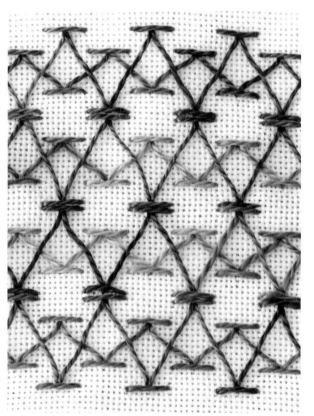

⸙ Lines of stepped chevron stitch worked row upon row to form a filling stitch

Coral Stitch

Coral stitch is an old embroidery stitch which creates a line that looks like a row of knots. It is used for outlines, as it follows a curve well.

1. Follow an imaginary line or use a pen that will disappear to mark a line. Bring the thread from the back of the fabric. Take a stitch at a slight right angle, above the line to be worked. Wrap the thread over, then under, the needle.

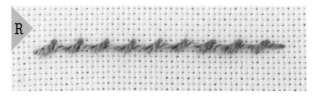

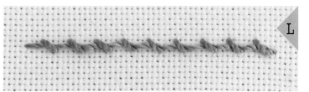

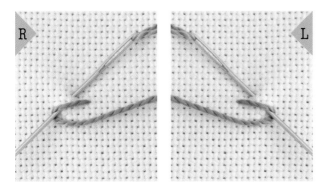

A line of coral stitch. This sample was worked using perle cotton #5. The effect created by coral stitch can be altered by using thicker threads or even a fine ribbon.

2. Pull the needle through the fabric to form a knot. Repeat the pattern along the line.

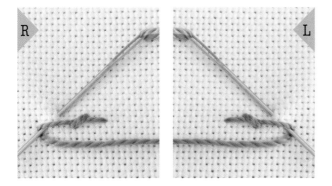

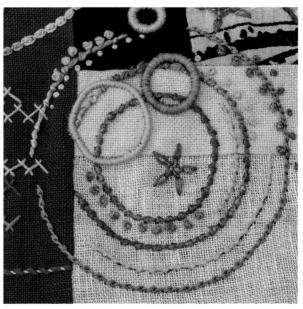

◊ Coral stitch used in a detail of a wall piece

Couching

Couching is wonderful technique that enables embroiderers to use interesting textured and novelty threads. You can create rich embellished surfaces and it is quick to work, and easy to do.

1. With couching, a surface thread is laid on the fabric, and anchored using a second thread. Use a large-eyed needle to bring the heavy thread through the fabric.

2. Using a finer needle and thread, make small, straight stitches over the thick thread to secure it to the fabric.

3. Continue until you have completed the line or filled the area.

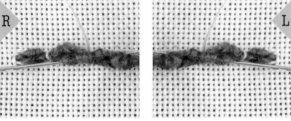

⸹ Usually, couching is done with thread in a matching color.
⸹ Here I used contrasting thread so you can see the stitching.

⸹ Couched threads and textured stitches. In this detail, I used
⸹ French knots (page 135), bullion knots (page 41), oyster stitch
⸹ (page 87), buttonhole wheels (page 68), and couching.

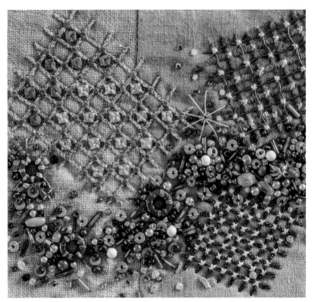

⸹ There are many ways to use couching. You can create
⸹ patterns and grids which are easily combined with other
⸹ stitches. I added cross-stitches at the intersections of each
⸹ couched thread.

Cretan Stitch

Cretan stitch—from the island of Crete—can be used in many decorative ways. With it you can fill a shape, create a border, or create a line.

1. Work from left (right to left for left-handed) to right between 2 imaginary horizontal lines. Bring the needle up through the fabric at the beginning, halfway between the upper and lower lines. Move along slightly, insert the needle on the top line and make a small stitch by pointing the needle to the center. Keeping the thread under the needle, pull it through the fabric.

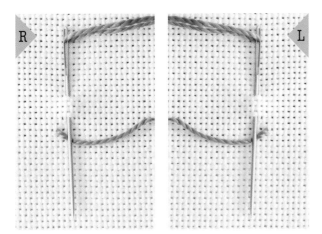

2. Move to the lower line and repeat the action.

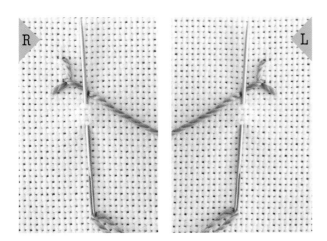

3. Continue working along the line. Make sure that with each small stitch the needle is pointed to the middle and the thread is under the needle as you pull it through.

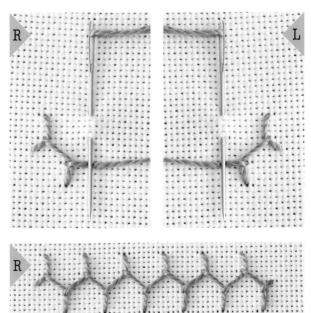

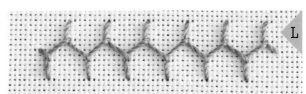

◇ A line of Cretan stitch

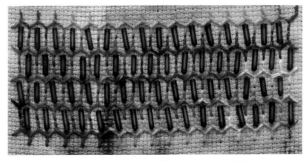

⧩ Perle cotton #8 on hand-painted Aida cloth, with bugle beads ⧩ between the stitches

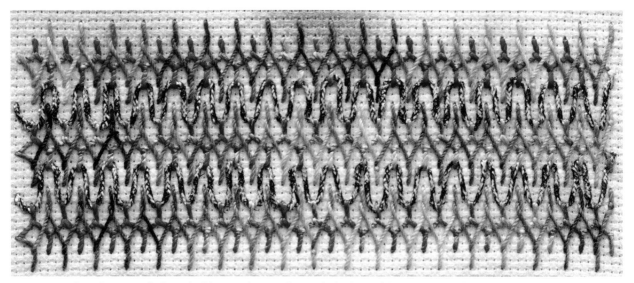

§ Cretan stitch works very well if you double it. In this sample I worked 3 lines of the stitch, then added another wider row on top.
§ Next, I laced the arms with a metallic thread.

◇ Four lines of Cretan stitch worked one on top of another.

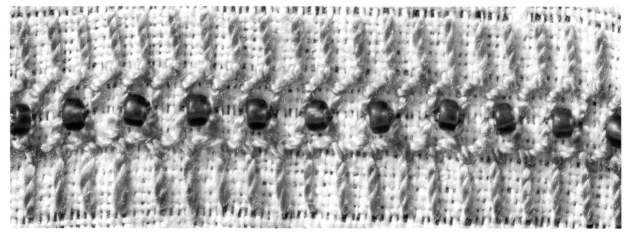

◇ Two rows of Cretan stitch worked face to face, but one side having a longer arm than the other. Beads were added along the middle.

§ Cretan stitch spaced closely together, with varied arm lengths to form a zigzag pattern. The Cretan
§ stitch is outlined in backstitch (page 33) with tulip stitches (page 91) in line.

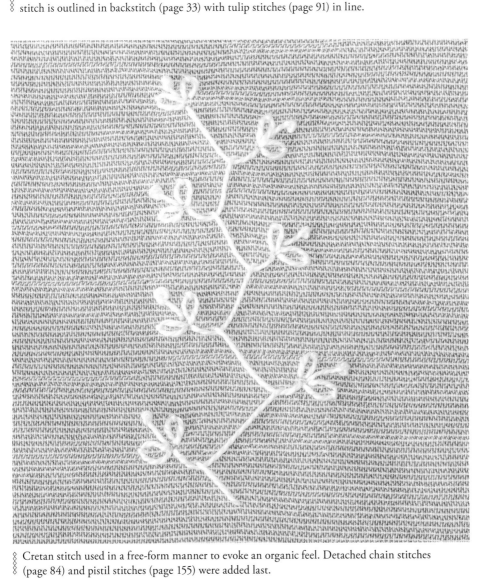

§ Cretan stitch used in a free-form manner to evoke an organic feel. Detached chain stitches
§ (page 84) and pistil stitches (page 155) were added last.

Cretan Stitch (Herringbone)

Cretan herringbone stitch is a combination of Cretan stitch (page 111) on one side of the line and herringbone stitch (page 136) on the other. Cretan herringbone stitch is a versatile stitch that can be worked in a regular or free-form manner and has many uses. For instance, you can use it for a border, as a fill, or along a curved line.

1. Work from left to right (right to left) between 2 imaginary lines. Start with half a Cretan stitch (page 111).

2. Move diagonally to the lower line and make half a herringbone stitch (page 136) by taking a small stitch to the left (right).

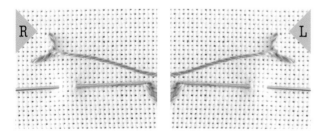

3. Pull your thread through. Move to the top of the line and make a small downward vertical stitch. Repeat these motions along the line.

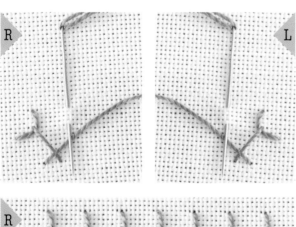

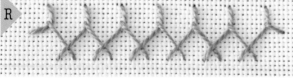

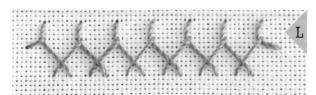

◇ A line of Cretan herringbone stitch

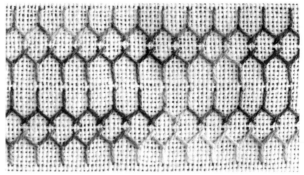

Pairs of Cretan herringbone stitch that have been worked face to face. Changes in the length of the arms of the Cretan part of the stitch and the width of the cross in the herringbone part of the stitch and the spacing allows for a large variety of patterns.

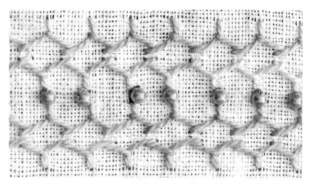

You can create some very rich borders by adding beads to the Cretan herringbone stitch.

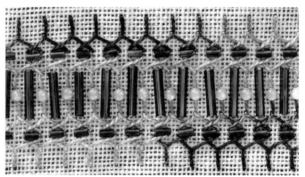

A border consisting of 4 lines of Cretan herringbone stitch worked in perle cotton #5, with beads added last

Cretan Stitch (Looped)

Looped Cretan stitch is interesting because you can change the spacing of the stitches to create different patterns. It is possible to vary the length, angle, and width of the wings to create interesting effects and beads are easily added.

1. Work from top to bottom between 2 imaginary horizontal lines. Bring the needle through the fabric at the start of the line on the top left (right) side. Insert the needle on the right (left) and make a stitch, keeping the thread under the needle.

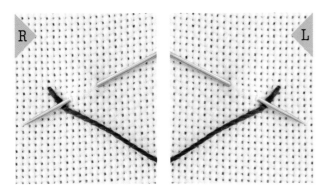

2. Pull the thread through the fabric. It should look like a shallow unsecured fly stitch (page 131). Insert the needle on the right (left) edge in the same place and make another small stitch. Keeping the thread under the needle, pull it through your fabric to create a loop. This extra loop gives this stitch its name.

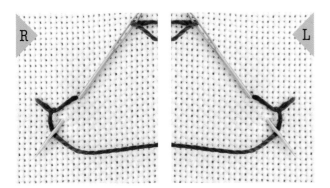

3. Move to the left (right) edge and make a small stitch. Keeping the thread under the needle, pull it through.

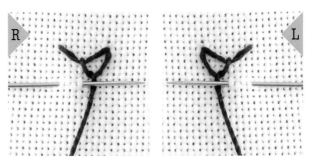

4. Insert your needle on the left (right) edge and make a small stitch. Keeping the thread under the needle, pull it through your fabric to create a loop.

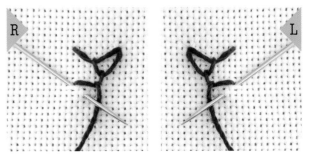

5. Move across to the right (left) and repeat this process. Continue working downward, back and forth until the line is worked.

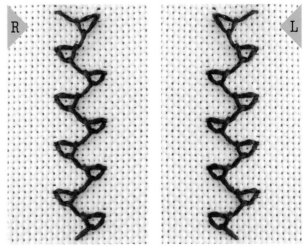

◊ Looped Cretan stitch

◇ Looped Cretan stitch worked in crazy quilting

Cross-Stitch

Cross-stitch is extremely quick and easy to work.

Work a diagonal straight stitch. Then work a second diagonal stitch laid in the opposite direction.

Although the construction of cross-stitch is the same, there are different ways of working. Cross-stitch can be worked individually, completing each cross before moving on to the next. Use this method if you are using a multicolored thread. Or you can work a line of half-cross-stitches, then finish the crosses on a return journey

No matter the method used, in traditional cross-stitch one rule remains constant. The top diagonals should always lie in the same direction. Although this rule is often deliberately broken by some contemporary embroiderers.

◇ A traditional cross-stitch motif used in crazy quilting

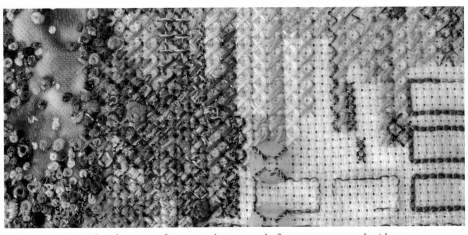

◇ A nontraditional free-form use of cross-stitch in a panel of contemporary embroidery

Cross-Stitch (Raised)

Raised cross-stitch is a quick and easy way to create little roselike flowers. It is created by working around a cross-stitch, whipping as you go. You can also use this as a silk ribbon stitch, and many novelty threads come to life with this stitch. You can also add a bead to the center of the flower.

1. First make a cross-stitch. The larger the cross, the larger the finished stitch.

2. Bring your needle out at the center of the cross, to the left (right) of the cross bar. Slide the needle under the bottom of the cross bar without picking up any fabric to whip the first spoke.

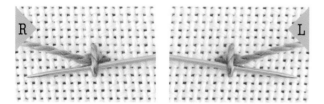

3. Move to the next bar of the cross and whip the next spoke.

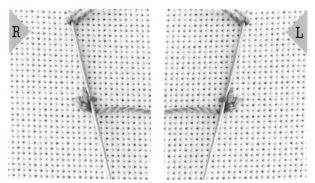

4. Continue around the cross in a counterclockwise (clockwise for left-handed) direction. As you work, pack the crossbars fairly firmly by pushing them to the center in order to create a neat little round disk. Continue working around the edge of the cross until the disk is well packed. Take the thread to the back and finish off.

◊ Whipped cross-stitch

◊ Raised cross-stitch used in crazy quilting, worked in synthetic knitting yarn.

Cross-Stitch (Woven)

This is a simple, quick, and very effective stitch, particularly if you experiment with the thread you use. For instance, it looks great as little flowers when you work it using silk ribbon. You can switch threads halfway through the process to use 2 different colors. The stitch looks fantastic with a bead in the middle.

1. Work a regular cross-stitch.

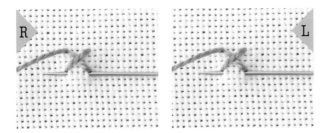

2. Make a third diagonal straight stitch in the same direction as the first stitch you worked.

3. To make the fourth straight stitch, weave the needle through the 2 bars and to the back of the fabric.

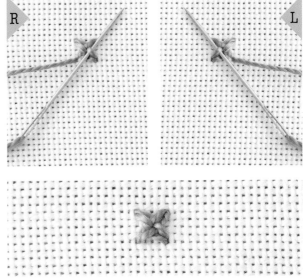

◊ Woven cross-stitch

◊ A detail with woven cross-stitch worked in wool alongside backstitch (page 33), French knots (page 135), and various beads.

Drizzle Stitch

Drizzle stitch is a three-dimensional stitch that stands free from the fabric. It is often used for the center of a flower, adding texture and dimension. It combines well with floral motifs and is useful in underwater scenes, as clusters of the stitch look like coral or sea anemones.

Since tension is important, stretch the fabric in an embroidery hoop or frame. This stitch is easier to work if you use a use a milliner's or straw needle, as the shaft of the needle is the same diameter as the eye, meaning you can slide the stitches along the needle easily in the second phase of the stitch. You can use any thread with a good twist, such as perle cotton.

1. Bring the threaded needle to the front of the fabric, then unthread the needle. Next to where the thread emerges, poke the needle a little way in the fabric. Wrap the thread over your index finger.

2. Rotate your finger, keeping the thread still over your finger but under slight tension. This movement will create a loop around your finger. Transfer the loop to the needle.

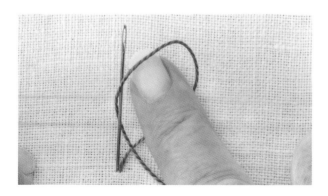

3. Slide the loop down the needle. Pull the thread until snug but not tight. This is the first cast-on stitch (page 78).

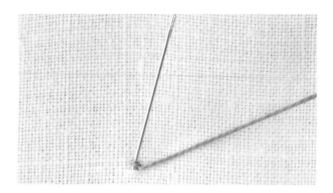

4. Work at least 6 loops, gently sliding them down the needle as you go. You can work 20 or 30 loops to create long spirals. Keep the stitches even on the needle.

5. When you have the required number of stitches, rethread the needle.

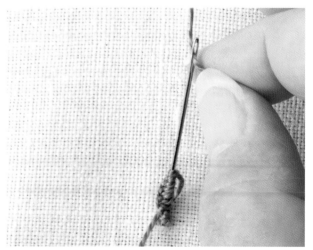

6. Gently pull the needle through the center of the cast on stitches and continue to pull the thread through the fabric to the back. Pull firmly but not too tight.

7. The finished stitch will be free at one end so that it will pop up from the fabric and will coil in a spiral to the base.

◊ Drizzle stitch

NOTE

The size of the stitch depends upon the number of cast-on stitches you use. The higher the number of cast on stitches, the bigger the loop. The thickness of the thread will determine the weight of the stitch.

◊ Drizzle stitch used in an underwater motif

Drizzle Stitch (Double)

Double drizzle stitch is another three-dimensional stitch that sits proud of the fabric. You can use any thread with a good twist, such as perle cotton. This stitch is easier to work if you use a use a milliner's or straw needle as the shaft of the needle is the same diameter as the eye, and this means you can easily slide the stitches along the needle in the second phase of the stitch.

1. Thread the needle with 2 threads. Bring the needle to the front of the fabric, then take the threads out of the needle. Place the needle in the fabric near to where the threads emerged.

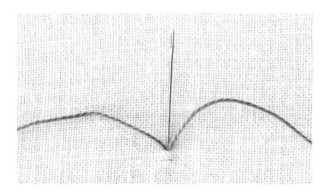

2. Place a single thread over your right (left) index finger and rotate your finger, creating a loop around your finger.

3. Transfer the loop from your finger to the needle.

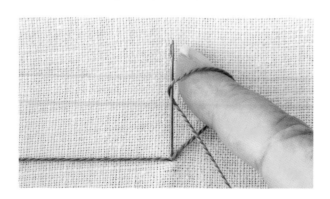

4. Gently slide the loop down the needle. This is the first cast-on stitch.

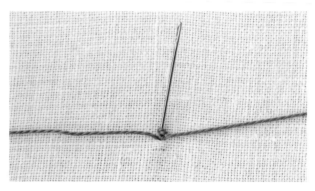

5. Pick up the second thread and repeat this cast-on action on the opposite side of the needle.

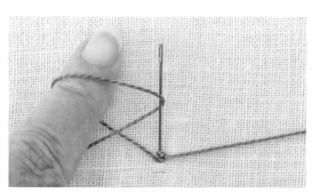

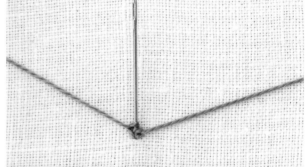

6. Continue adding stitches to alternate sides of the needle.

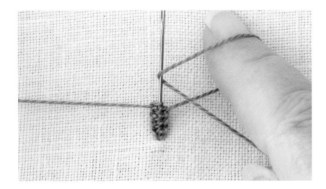

7. Make 8–10 cast-on stitches, keeping the stitches as even as you can.

8. Rethread the needle.

9. Hold the stitches while you pull the threaded needle through the center of the stitches to the back of the fabric.

10. You have a stitch that stands proud! The finished stitch is free at one end so that it will pop up from the fabric. The size of the stitch depends upon the number of cast-on stitches you use. The higher the number of cast-on stitches, the bigger the loop. The thickness of the thread will determine the weight of the stitch.

◇ Double drizzle stitch

◇ Double drizzle stitch used on a crazy quilting seam

Feather Stitch

Feather stitch is a versatile stitch that can hold a curve, making it ideal to use in any organic motif, such as floral sprays, vines, and twisting twiglike stems. It also looks great in underwater scenes, as the flowing lines are very suitable to represent corals and seaweed.

Tips

- To make sure this stitch sits neatly on a curve, keep the center of the stitch on the line you want to follow.

- You can vary feather stitch by changing the width between the tops of the Y, the angle of your needle, and changes of spacing in the length of stitches.

1. Bring the thread up at the top left (right for left-handed). Insert the needle to the right (left) and make a downward stitch so that the needle emerges between the 2 points. With the thread wrapped under the needle, pull it through the fabric. It should make a V.

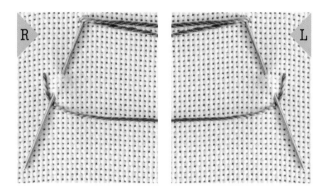

2. Insert the needle to the right (left) and make another downward diagonal stitch so that the needle emerges between the 2 points. With the thread wrapped under the needle, pull it through the fabric.

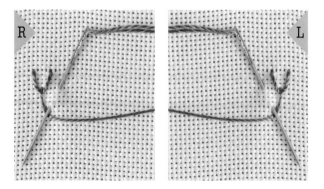

3. Continue working on alternate sides of the line, keeping the Vs aligned.

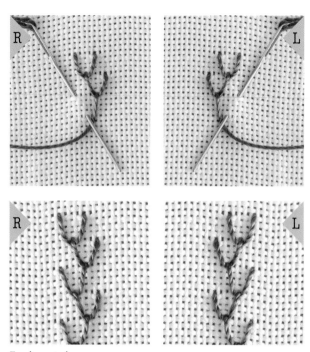

Feather stitch

A small marine design where feather stitch dominates. I used a variety of threads including novelty yarns such as eyelash thread, chenille, and chainette.

In this sample, the legs are different lengths. Rows were worked back to back then beads added. The result looks very different from regular feather stitch.

Feather Stitch (and Chain)

You have many possibilities with this combination of stitches. For instance, you can vary the length of the chain stitch, or work rows back to back. Many of the variations of both chain stitch and feather stitch can be adapted to this stitch.

1. Make 2 feather stitches (page 124).

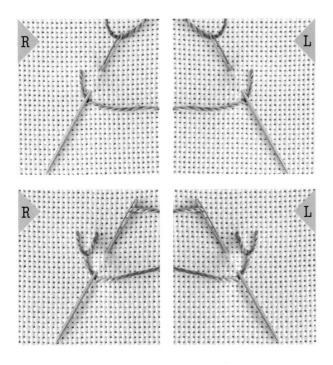

2. Insert the needle at the base of the second feather stitch and wrap the thread under your needle, to make a chain stitch (page 80). Pull the needle through.

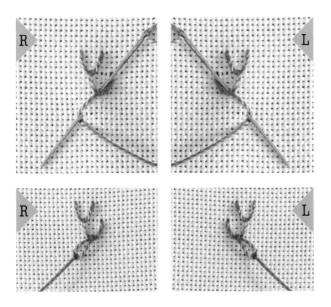

3. Move to the right side of the line and continue with feather stitch.

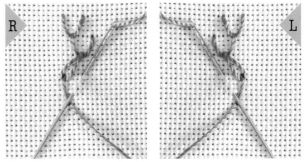

4. Work down the row repeating this pattern.

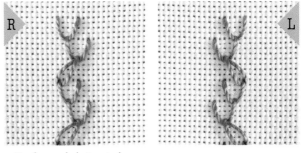

◇ Feather and chain stitch

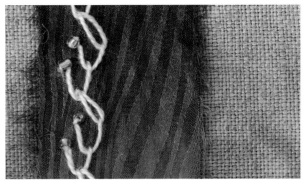

◇ Feather and chain stitch worked in perle cotton #5

⸙ In this crazy quilt block seam, a bead is added to the middle of the chain stitch.

Feather Stitch (Knotted)

Knotted feather stitch can create ornate patterns and effects by varying the spacing between the arms and spine length. Add beads for a more decorative line.

1. Work this stitch from top to bottom. For beginners, it is useful to imagine 4 parallel lines; you may find it useful to mark the fabric with guidelines using a water dissolvable marker or fade-out fabric marker. Bring the needle out at the top of the line to be worked. Insert the needle a little to the right (left for left-handed) on the same level and make a small downward stitch, keeping the thread under the needle point. Pull the thread through.

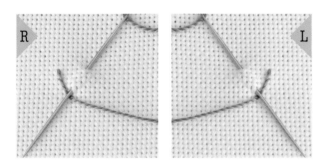

2. Pass the needle under the thread at the right (left) side of the V shape. Do not pick up any fabric. Wrap the working thread under the needle point as though working a chain stitch (page 80).

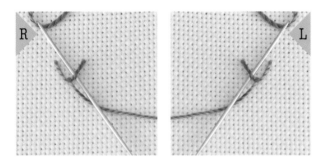

3. Pull the needle under the foundation thread so that you are working a small chain stitch on the bar.

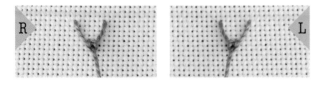

4. Insert the needle to the right (left) on the same level as the chain stitch you just made.

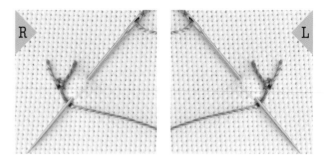

5. Continue until the line is complete.

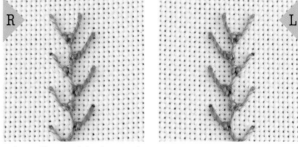

A line of knotted feather stitch

Knotted feather stitch on a piece of crazy quilting with beads and cast-on stitch (page 78) flowers.

Knotted feather stitch in perle cotton #5 with detached chain stitch (page 84) flowers.

Feather Stitch (Plaited)

This stitch is simple but versatile and can be very effective if you experiment with different spacing and yarns.

1. Work plaited feather stitch between 2 imaginary vertical lines. Bring the needle out at the top of the left (right for left-handed) line. Reinsert it a little to the right and make a downward stitch.

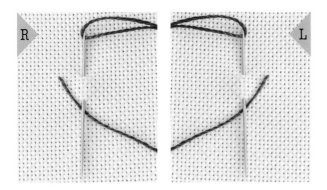

2. Keeping the thread under the needle point, pull the thread through the fabric to make the first stitch. Insert the needle to the left (right), in line with the base of the V you have just made and make a vertical stitch.

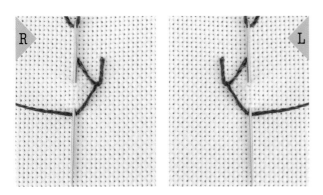

3. Pull the thread through the fabric. Work these movements alternately down the line to complete the first row of a feather stitch with straight sides.

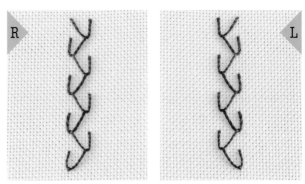

4. For demonstration purposes the second journey is worked in red thread. Bring the thread out at the top of the second stitch. Insert the needle top left (right), and have the needle come out where it first emerged. This stitch exists in order to start the row neatly.

5. To make the first V, insert the needle at the base of the first stitch. With the thread under the needle, pull the thread through.

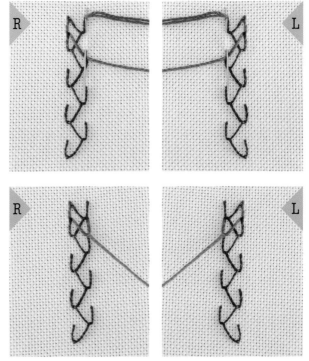

6. Slide the needle under the cross bar to the left (right).

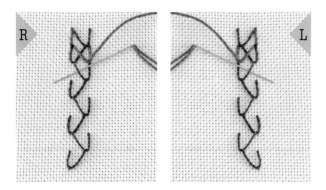

7. Once again, take a downward vertical stitch in the open space of the left (right) side. Pull the needle through.

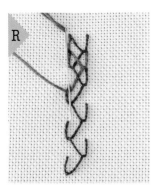

8. Repeat these movements, alternating down the line. In every second stitch, take your thread under the cross bar of the first row of stitches.

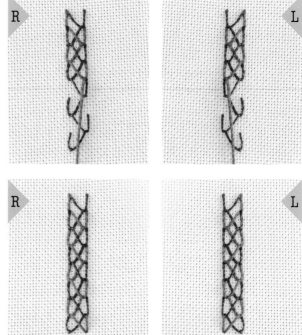

◇ Plaited feather stitch

◇ Plaited feather stitch worked in variegated perle cotton #5 on a crazy quilt block

◊ Plaited feather stitch worked in 2 colors of perle cotton #5 on a crazy quilt block

◊ Plaited feather stitch worked in 2 colors of perle cotton #5.

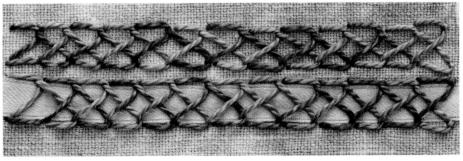

◊ Plaited feather stitch used to couch down a ribbon

Feather Stitch (Triangular)

Triangular feather stitch looks a little complex. But once in the swing of it, you will find it quick and easy.

1. Work 2 regular feather stitches (page 124).

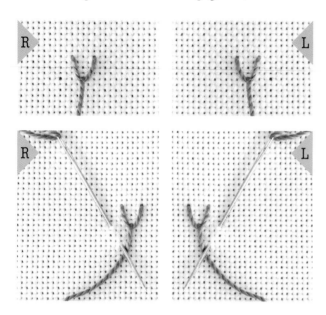

2. Insert the needle where the thread emerged on the first feather stitch and take a straight downward stitch. The needle should emerge lower than the base of the second feather stitch.

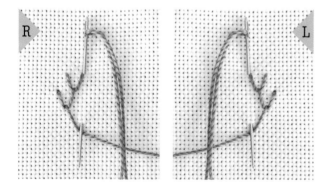

3. With the thread under the needle, pull the needle through.

4. Move the needle to the left (right) and create the next V stitch.

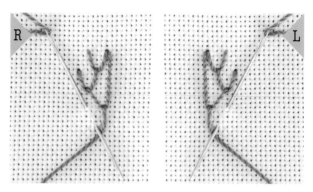

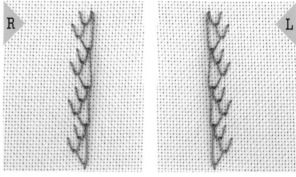

5. Continue to finish the line.

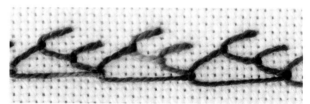

◊ Triangular feather stitch

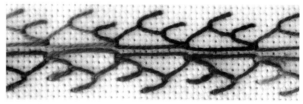

◊ A single line of triangular feather stitch

◊ Two lines of triangular feather stitch worked back to back

Fly Stitch

Fly stitch is versatile, and quick and easy to work. You can use this stitch in a regular or free-form manner. It also is known as *Y stitch* and *open loop stitch*.

1. Bring the thread up at the top left (right for left-handed) and insert the needle to the right (left). Make a downward stitch between the top 2 points.

2. With the thread wrapped under the needle, pull it through the fabric. Secure the V in position with a small vertical straight stitch.

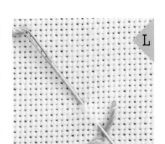

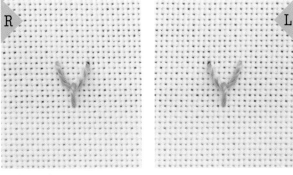

◇ Fly stitch

⸙ Fly stitch worked free-form over layers of net and chiffon to create a watery effect

⸙ Fly stitch in a pattern alongside detached chain stitch (page 80)

Fly Stitch (var. Crown Stitch)

Crown stitch is an isolated stitch that you can sprinkle across an area to produce a delicate texture. You can build up patterns with crown stitch, and it lends itself to being worked in a wide variety of thread.

1. Start with a fly stitch (page 131).

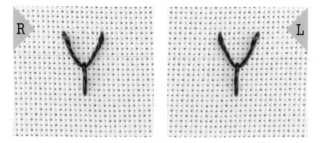

2. Add 2 slanting straight stitches at the base.

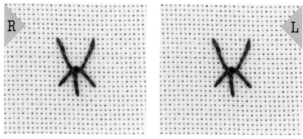

◇ Crown stitch

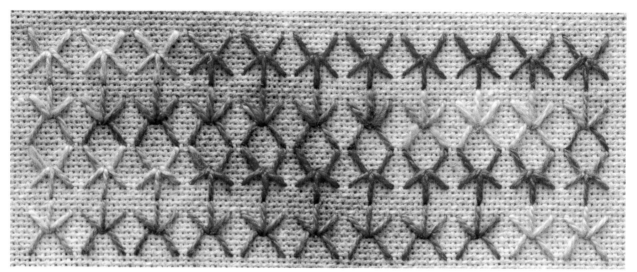

§ Crown stitch is arranged in rows to create a patterned fill. You can work the stitch in a variety of widths and heights by changing the height of the arms. You can make interesting variations by working it in rows closer together or further apart.

Fly Stitch (Laced)

Laced fly stitch produces a branched line with a central braidlike section. You can vary this stitch by changing the angle of the V on the foundation stitches. The lacing thread can also be of a different weight, color, or type.

1. Work a foundation row of fly stitch (page 131).

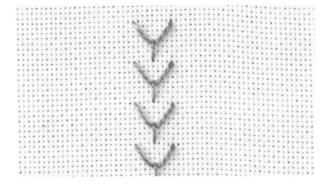

2. Lace a second contrasting thread, starting at the bottom.

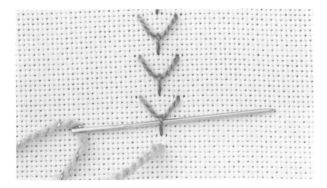

Tips

• Use a blunt-ended tapestry needle for the second thread so you do not split the foundation threads as you sew.

• Do not pass the needle through the background fabric.

⚬ Laced fly stitch worked in perle cotton #5 and laced with a metallic thread.

3. Pass it in the other direction under the tie of the next fly stitch.

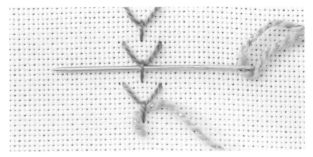

4. Continue lacing to the top.

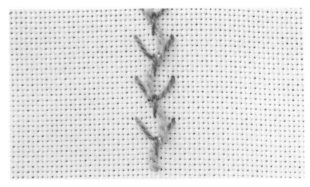

5. Turn the lacing thread and repeat the lacing movement down the other side of the fly stitches.

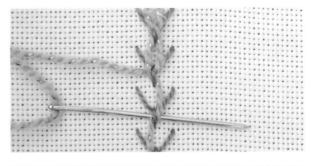

⚬ In this line of laced fly stitch, the fly stitches are in perle cotton #5 and the lacing is in a 4-ply knitting yarn.

Fly Stitch (Reversed)

Reversed fly stitch is an example of an isolated stitch that is first duplicated, then arranged in patterns. It is easy and quick to work, which makes it enjoyable to experiment with. You can change the angle of the fly stitch arms to create varieties. The completed unit can be duplicated and arranged in patterns along a line or around a circle.

1. Start with a single fly stitch (page 131).

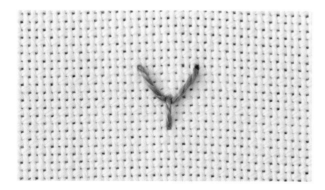

2. Turn your work and make a second fly stitch. Line it up so that the second stitch is worked on top of the first.

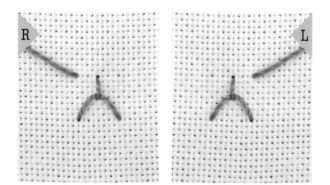

3. Make sure the center of both V's line up together.

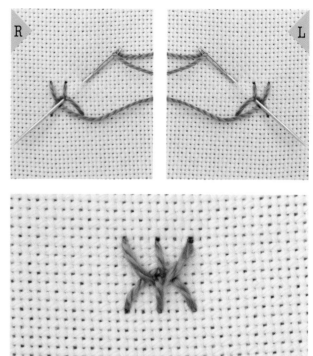

◇ Reversed fly stitch

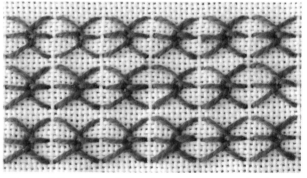

◇ Reversed fly stitch worked perle cotton #5 arranged in lines

French Knot

French knots are very handy; you are likely to use them everywhere. The thickness of the thread and the number of wraps on the needle will determine the size of the finished knot.

1. Twist the needle around the thread 2 or 3 times and take the needle back into the fabric, 1 or 2 threads away from where the thread first emerged.

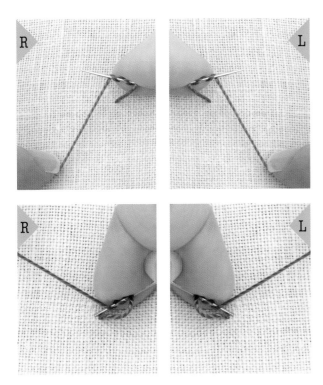

2. Brush the knot down the shaft of the needle with the nail of your left (right for left-handed) thumb so that it is sitting firmly on the fabric. Take the needle through to the back of the fabric.

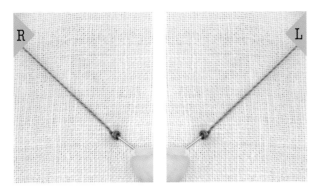

3. Use your left (right) index finger to hold the thread against the fabric as you pull the thread through the knot. This helps prevent tangles.

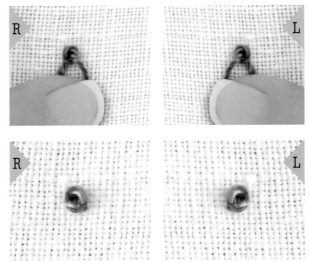

◇ The completed knot

Tips

• If your knot pops through the fabric, leave a bigger gap between where the thread emerges from the fabric, and where it goes back in.

• If your wraps get stuck on the needle, use a milliners needle, which has an eye that is the same width as the shaft of the needle. The knot will slide off the needle easily.

French knots are heavily used alongside buttonhole wheels (page 68), bullion knots (page 41), cast-on stitch (page 78), oyster stitch (page 87), whipped wheel (page 183), and whipped spoke stitch (page 181).

Herringbone Stitch

Herringbone's structure forms regular patterns, which makes it ideal to work row upon row, or to play with combinations of offset lines of stitches. It can be doubled up, overlapped, or even divided into sections and rearranged, as in herringbone square (page 144). It also can be laced as in twisted lattice band (page 146). Since it forms a band, you can use it to couch down ribbons, braids, and novelty yarns. Herringbone is a very versatile stitch!

1. Work along 2 imaginary horizontal lines. Bring the needle out on the top left. Move diagonally to the lower line and make a small stitch.

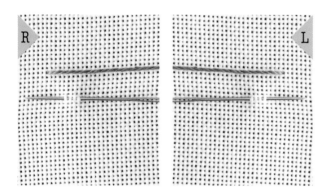

2. Insert the thread on the upper line, a little to the right (left), and make a small stitch.

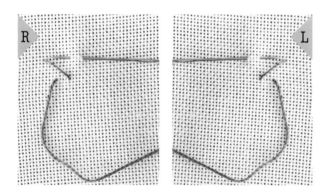

3. Continue the pattern along the line

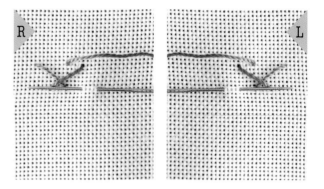

◇ A completed row of herringbone stitch

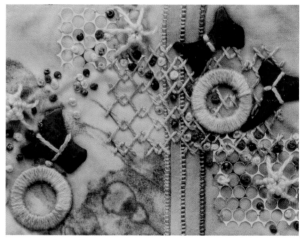

§ Detail of a wall piece where herringbone sits as a grid behind
§ a feature of coconut beads and wrapped metal washers

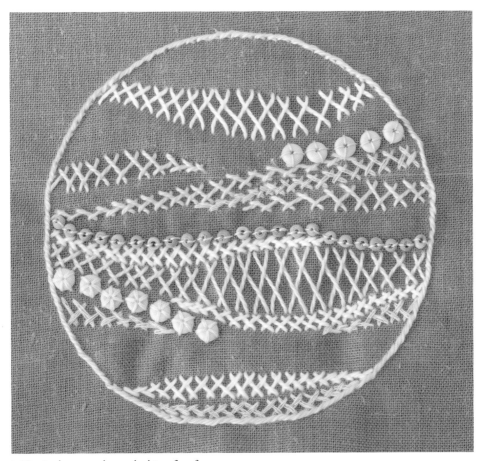

◊ Herringbone can be worked in a free-form manner.

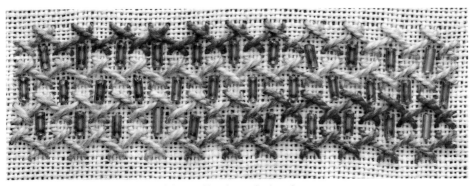

◊ Herringbone row upon row, with lines of beads stitched in the spaces

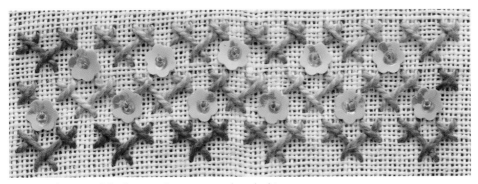

◊ Herringbone stitch broken into basic units and worked in a pattern

Herringbone Stitch (Barred)

Barred herringbone is a quick and easy stitch that can be used as a border or worked line upon line as a filling.

1. Work a line of herringbone stitch (page 136).

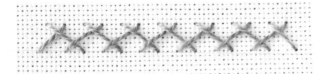

2. Work vertical lines from the edge of the top cross to the edge of the bottom cross. I have worked this step in a different colored thread so the bars can be seen easily.

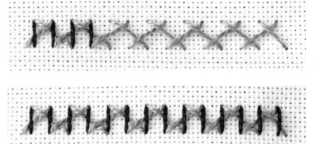

◇ A line of barred herringbone stitch

◇ Barred herringbone worked in variegated perle cotton #8

◇ Barred herringbone worked in variegated silk thread with bugle beads added last

◇ Barred herringbone can also be used as a pulled stitch. Here it is worked in perle cotton #8.

Herringbone Stitch (Buttonholed)

Buttonholed herringbone starts with a foundation of herringbone stitch, which is then buttonholed.

Tips

• Use a blunt-ended needle for the second thread so that you do not split the foundation herringbone stitches.

• Use a fairly solid thread, such as perle cotton #5.

1. Work a line of herringbone (page 136). Bring your needle out at the base of the row.

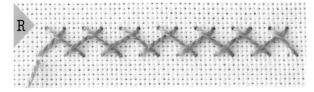

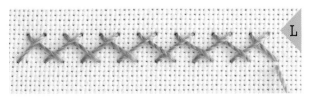

2. Work a buttonhole stitch (page 43) on the bar of the first herringbone stitch. **Note:** Do not pass the needle through the fabric; use the herringbone stitches as the foundation.

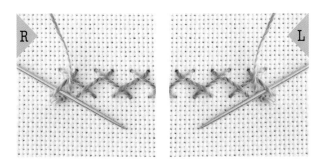

3. Work buttonhole stitches along the bar until they are snug.

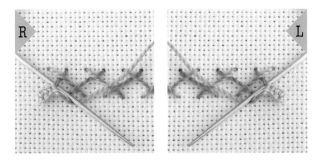

4. When you reach the top of the bar, pass the needle under the cross of the herringbone stitch and work a single buttonhole stitch.

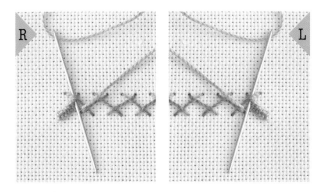

5. Continue the buttonhole stitch on the downward bar until the foundation stitches of herringbone are covered.

6. Continue the pattern. At each cross bar, work 1 buttonhole stitch to make each section neat.

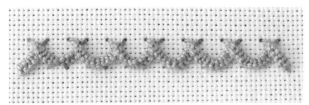

◇ Buttonholed herringbone

◇ A line of buttonholed herringbone used in crazy quilting

Herringbone Stitch (Double)

This version of double herringbone stitch can be laced easily. Since the stitches are plaited, it holds a secondary lacing thread neatly, such as in twisted lattice band (page 146).

1. Lay a foundation row of herringbone stitch (page 136).

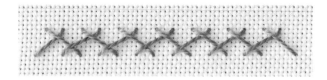

2. Work a second row of herringbone. On every second stitch, slide the needle under the cross bar created by the first row of stitches. This means that the second row of herringbone is woven or interlaced through the first row.

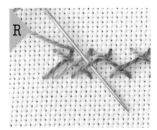 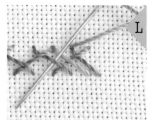

3. The pattern is to take the needle over on the upward stitch, and under on the downward stitch.

 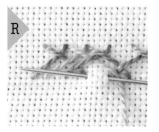

4. Continue along the line. This variety looks very effective when worked in 2 colors.

◊ A line of double herringbone stitch

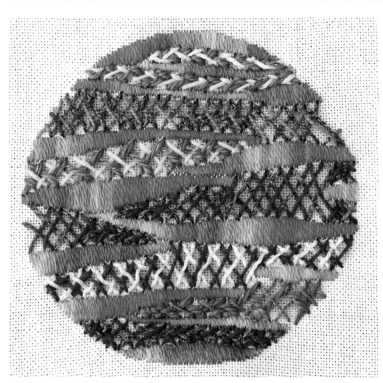

◊ Double herringbone worked free-form

Herringbone Stitch (Laced Square)

You can work laced herringbone square as an isolated stitch or arranged in patterns. Since the lacing process does not involve many passes of the needle through the fabric, you can experiment with thicker novelty threads and yarns.

Tip If your work puckers because of tension in the lacing, use a hoop or frame.

1. Work a herringbone square (page 144).

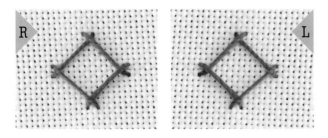

2. Bring your needle up on the inside left (right for left-handed) corner. Pass the needle under the crossed foundation bars of the top corner of the square. Do not go through the fabric as you are lacing, not stitching.

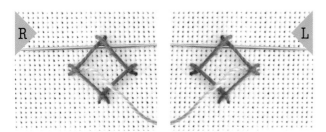

3. Pass the needle under the crossed foundation bars at the right (left) corner.

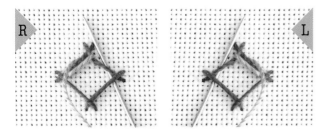

4. Continue around the square.

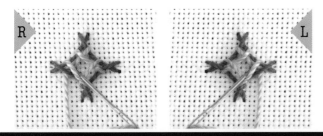

5. Secure the laced square with 4 crossed straight stitches. Start by bringing the thread from the back and making a straight stitch across the laced square.

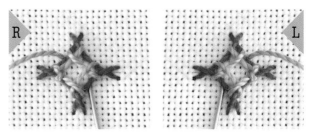

6. Repeat the straight stitch on the other sides so you have 2 straight stitches making a cross.

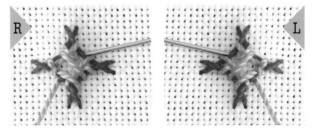

7. Bring your needle out and work 2 more stitches to complete a double cross-stitch.

◇ A completed laced herringbone square

Herringbone Stitch (Raised Band)

Raised herringbone band is built in layers—first satin stitch, then herringbone, then lacing. It looks complex but is relatively simple. You can vary the width of the band and change threads. It makes a very effective border and is quite complete in itself. You can also work the band on a gentle curve.

1. Lay down a band of satin stitch (page 161).

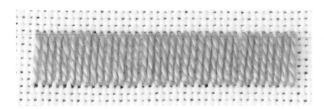

2. Work a line of herringbone stitch (page 136). Make sure the herringbone stitches are slightly loose, as lacing will tighten the stitches.

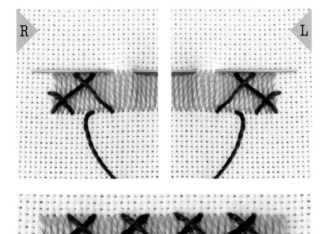

3. To lace the herringbone stitches, bring the needle out at the side of the row. Thread the needle under the herringbone.

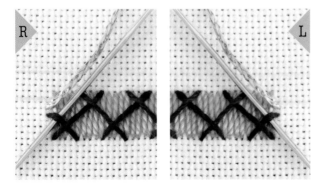

4. Take the lacing thread over the crossed bars and up under the next diagonal line.

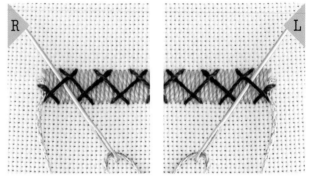

5. Repeat this motion along the line of herringbone. Don't pull too tight; just relax and lace the threads.

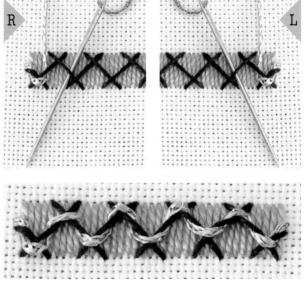

◇ A line of raised herringbone band

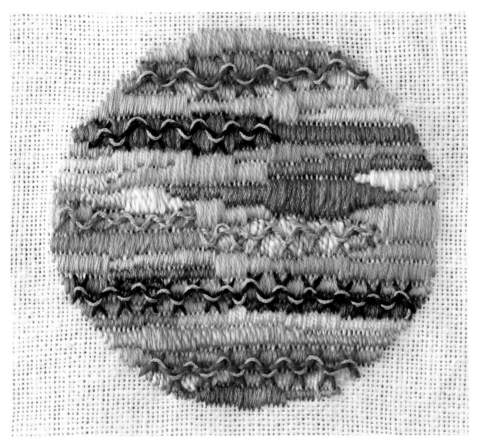

§ Raised herringbone band and satin stitch (page 161) worked free-form using cotton, silk, stranded
§ cotton floss, wool, and metallic threads

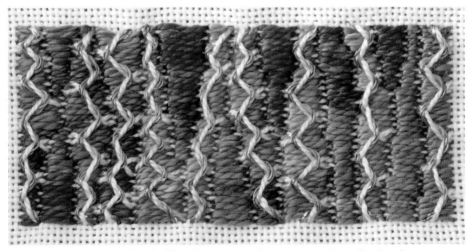

◊ Raised herringbone band worked free-form using perle cotton #5 and metallic threads

Herringbone Stitch (Square)

Herringbone square stitch is simply herringbone stitch (page 136) worked in a square. You can use it as an isolated motif or arrange the units in patterns so that it becomes an interesting filler.

1. Starting on the left (right for left-handed) side of the square, take your needle up diagonally, and make a small horizontal stitch. This is the first corner of the square.

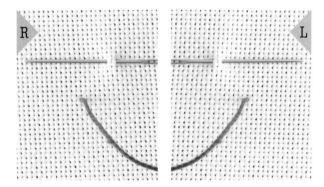

2. Take your needle diagonally down and make a small vertical stitch. This is the second corner of the square.

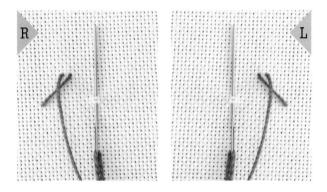

3. To make the third corner of the square, take the needle diagonally downward and make a small horizontal stitch.

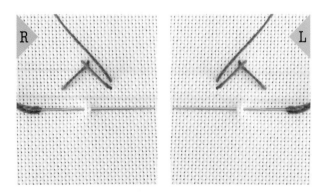

4. Take the needle back up to the first corner to complete the stitch.

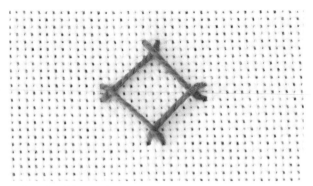

◊ Completed herringbone square

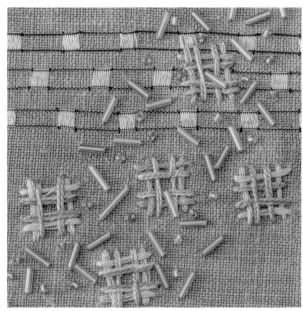

§ Free-form herringbone squares stacked in combination with couched eyelash thread and beads

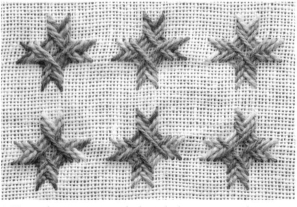

§ Herringbone squares stacked, worked in a variegated cotton thread

Herringbone Stitch (Tied)

Tied herringbone is a highly decorative composite stitch that consists of herringbone stitch that has been tied with a straight stitch where the bars cross. You can switch out the straight tacking stitch for other decorative stitches. This stitch is also known as tacked herringbone.

Work a line of herringbone stitch (page 136), then tack down the crosses. You can substitute the straight stitches for cross-stitches or detached chain stitches (page 84). Other nice tacking stitches are fly stitch (page 131), oyster stitch (page 87), bullion knots (page 41), or beads.

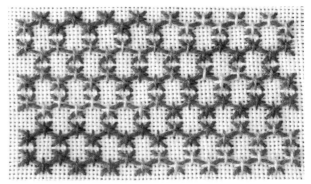

Rows of herringbone worked in perle cotton #5 tied with crosses worked in variegated perle cotton #8.

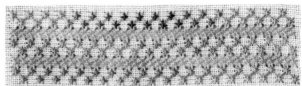

Lines of herringbone tied with a cross, interspersed with herringbone stitches worked closely together. The sample was worked in variegated perle cotton #8.

Two lines of tied herringbone worked as a border in hand-dyed perle cotton #5. Sequins were stitched in the spaces of the pattern.

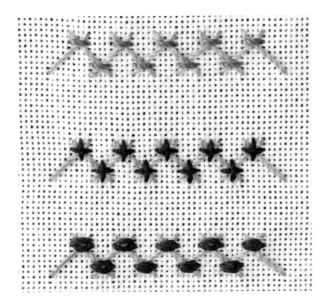

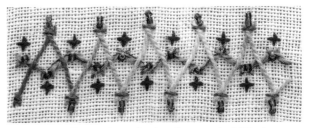

Two rows of herringbone that have been stacked. The bottom row was worked in wool and tied with a seed bead. The top row is tied with the straight stitch. Seed beads were added in the fork of the cross.

◇ Two lines of tied herringbone

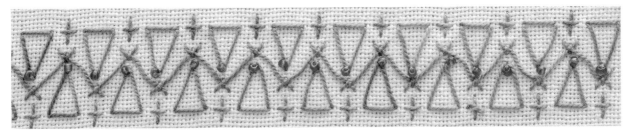

◇ Tied herringbone tied with an upright straight stitch

Herringbone Stitch (Twisted Lattice Band)

Twisted lattice band creates an attractive band of stitching that can be used as a border. You can also work this stitch row upon row to create an interesting filling.

1. Lay a foundation row of herringbone stitch (page 136). Space the stitches slightly wider and looser than normal. The lacing will tighten the stitches slightly, and if you space the foundation stitches a little wider, it gives you room for thicker threads if you want to use them.

2. Work a second row of herringbone stitch. On every second stitch, slide the needle under the cross bar created by the first row of stitches. The pattern is to take the needle under on the downward stitch and over on the upward stitch.

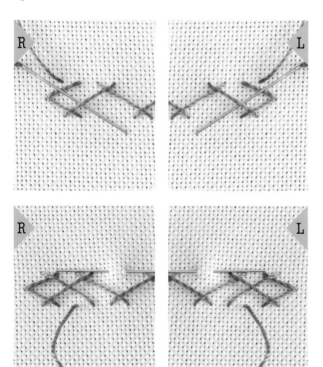

3. Complete a line of double herringbone stitch, spaced between the foundation row.

The lacing is worked in 2 journeys. Please note the weaving in twisted lattice band will not work if you do not use this version of double herringbone, as you need the woven cross bars for the lacing thread to sit neatly. Use a tapestry needle to avoid splitting the foundation herringbone stitch.

4. Bring the needle out at the start of the row and slide it under the first bar pointing left (right for left-handed). Pull the thread under the stitch.

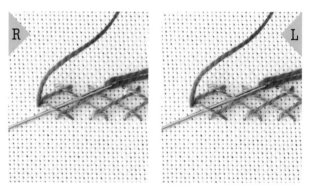

5. Slide the needle under the second bar and pull the thread under the stitch.

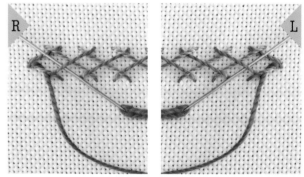

6. Continue along the line. Take care to lace, and not to pick up any of the fabric.

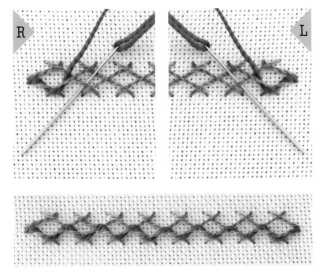

7. Turn your work and lace along the other side of the row.

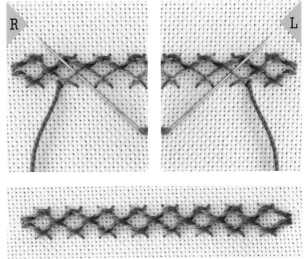

◇ Completed twisted lattice band

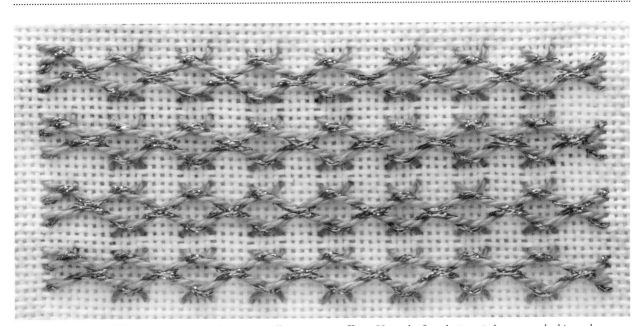

Experiment with different threads to develop some really interesting effects. Here, the foundation stitches are worked in perle cotton #5 and then laced with a metallic thread.

Needle-Woven Picot

Needle-woven picot is a fun three-dimensional stitch that is ideal for leaves and flower petals. You can work this stitch short or long for different-size leaves. When worked wide and stacked, they form lichen-type textures. If worked stacked in semicircles, they make great pine cones!

Tip Use a blunt tapestry needle so that you do not split the threads as you weave them.

1. Place a pin in your work with the pin emerging from the fabric where you want the base of your picot to be. Bring the thread out at the base to the left (right for left-handed) of the pin. Take the thread back into the fabric on the right hand side placing the loop under the pin.

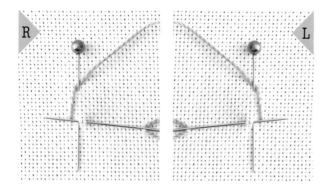

2. Bring the thread out, at the base of where the pin emerges.

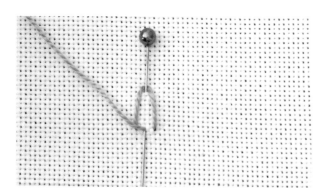

3. Wrap the thread behind the pin, from right to left.

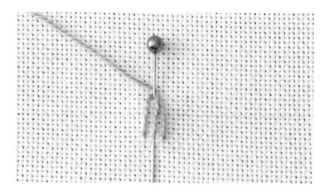

4. Begin weaving by sliding the needle from left to right, picking up the 2 outer threads. You do not pick up the middle thread.

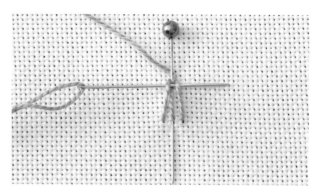

5. Pull the thread through firmly but not too tight. Turn the needle and slide the needle under the middle thread.

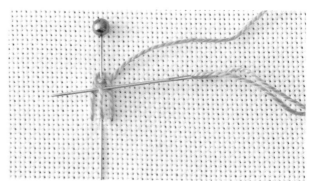

6. Pull your thread through and continue in this back-and-forth motion. As you weave, use the needle to pack the picot so that it is firm.

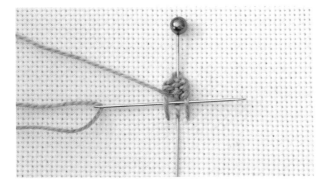

7. Continue weaving until the picot is packed firmly to the base. Take the thread to the back and secure with 2 small backstitches.

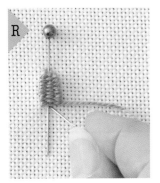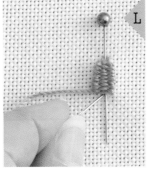

8. Remove the pin, and you have a freestanding needle-woven picot which pops up from the fabric.

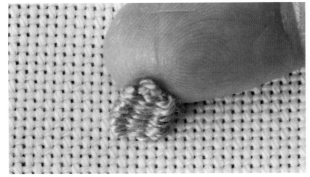

◇ Completed needle-woven picot

◇ Needle-woven picot in a floral motif

Palestrina Stitch

Palestrina stitch will produce an interesting textured line that will hold a curve well, which means it can be used to outline shapes in a design. A firm twisted thread, such as perle cotton, will show the knots to their best advantage.

1. Bring the needle up through the fabric and make a small diagonal stitch. This forms the first bar onto which the stitch is made.

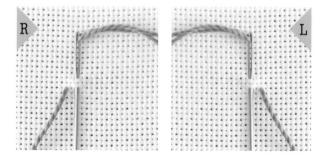

2. Pass the needle under the stitch. This movement will take your thread over the top of the bar. Pull the thread through.

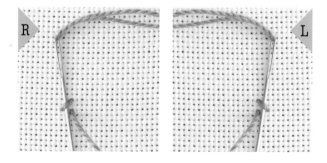

3. Pass the needle under the bar a second time. Loop the thread under the needle and pull the needle under the bar.

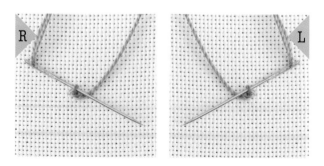

4. Pull the thread snug to form a knot.

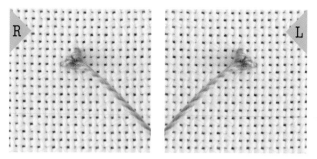

5. Move along the line and make a second bar onto which you work your knot.

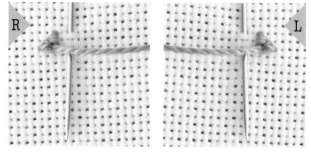

6. Space the knots evenly and close together to produce a textured line.

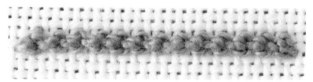

◊ Palestrina stitch

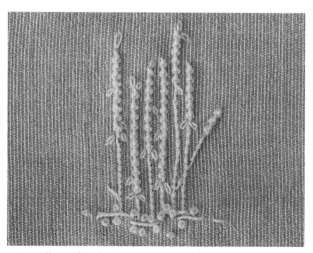

◊ A small motif worked in perle cotton #5

Pekinese Stitch

Pekinese stitch is also known as Chinese stitch, since it is found on Chinese embroideries, worked in silk, row upon row, sometimes 30–40 stitches to the inch.

Pekinese stitch creates a heavy line which can follow a curve well. This stitch is useful as a finishing line around the edge of items like fabric postcards, fabric book pages, needle books, or pincushions. For extra interest, experiment with different threads. You can lace with fine cord, chainette, rayon ribbon floss, a yarn, or a fine ribbon.

1. Work a foundation line of backstitch (page 33) in a loose manner, because the threading will tighten the stitches.

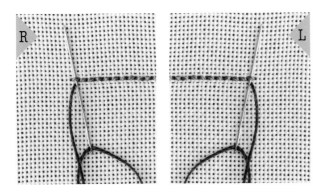

Tip Use a blunt-tipped tapestry needle for the second pass to avoid splitting the foundation stitches.

2. Using a second, decorative thread, lace the thread up through the first stitch, then down through the third. Do not pass the needle through the fabric.

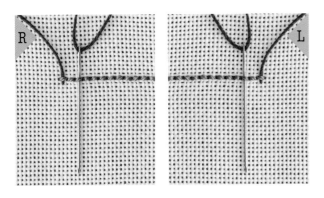

3. Move back 1 stitch and lace the thread up, then down through the fourth stitch.

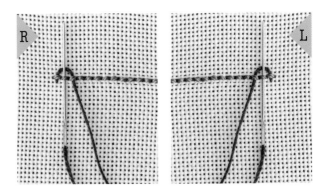

4. Repeat this lacing process along the line. Tighten slightly after each threaded loop.

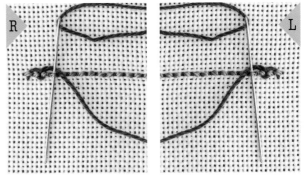

◇ A line of Pekinese stitch

⚜ Pekinese stitch used along the edge of lace on a crazy quilt block

Pekinese Stitch (Chained)

Chained Pekinese creates a great border and takes on a life of its own once you start working it in 2 rows face to face or back to back. It also lends itself to experimenting with different threads in contrasting color and texture.

To work chained Pekinese stitch, you need to understand how to work Pekinese stitch (page 151).

Tip Weave the second thread using a blunt-ended tapestry needle to avoid splitting the foundation threads.

1. Start by working a row of backstitches (page 33) looser than usual. Below the line, space a line of vertical straight stitches so that a stitch sits between each pair of backstitches.

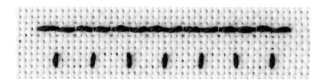

2. Bring your needle out at the base of the line of back-stitches. Slide the needle up, under the second backstitch. Pull the thread through.

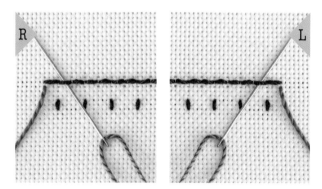

3. To make the first "chain," slide the needle under the previous backstitch and pull the thread through.

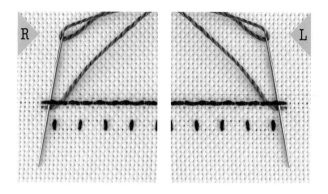

4. Slide the needle under the little straight stitch and pull your thread through.

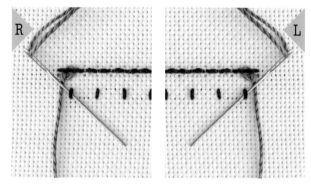

5. Slide the needle under the next backstitch in the top line. Pull your thread through.

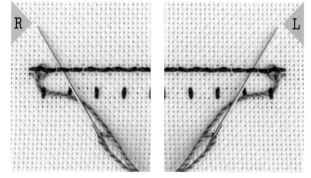

6. Slide the needle under the previous backstitch and the next small straight stitch and pull the thread through to complete the first loop of chained Pekinese stitch.

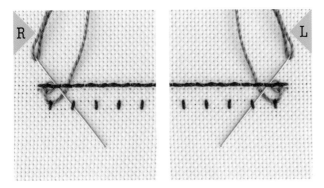

7. Continue the pattern using the vertical stitches to catch the "chain" of every second loop.

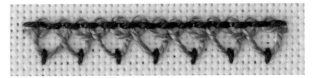

◇ Chained Pekinese

◇ A single line of chained Pekinese

◇ Two lines of chained Pekinese stitch worked face to face

◇ Chained Pekinese used on a crazy quilt block

Pekinese Stitch (Diminishing)

Diminishing Pekinese is worked on a foundation of backstitches. However, unlike regular Pekinese stitch, the foundation stitches are worked in a variety of shapes, including circles.

1. Work a number of foundation rows of backstitch (page 33) in a simple shape. The rows of backstitch should line up vertically and be worked in a fairly loose manner because the threading will tighten them.

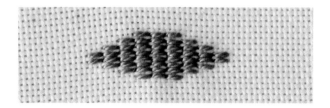

2. To thread, start at the narrowest point. Pass the needle under the stitches, not through the fabric.

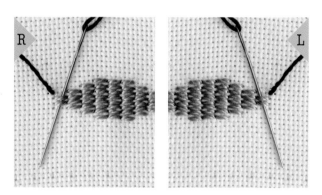

3. Slide the needle under the third row of stitches, then back through the second row.

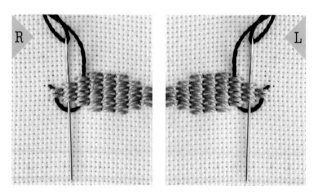

4. Repeat this back and forward motion, lacing the foundation stitches along the shape.

◊ Diminishing Pekinese stitch used in a traditional motif

◊ Diminishing Pekinese stitch used in crazy quilting

Pistil Stitch

Pistil stitch looks like a French knot with a tail. It is an interesting stitch, ideal to use for the center of flowers or arranged in a circle as a flower motif. The weight of the thread will determine the size of the finished stitch.

Tip This stitch is easier to work with the fabric stretched in an embroidery hoop. I recommend that you use a milliners needle.

1. Bring the thread to the front of the fabric. Wrap the thread twice around the needle.

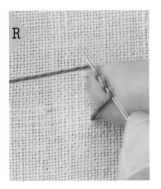 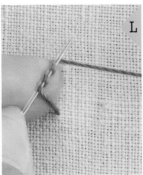

2. Insert the needle back into the fabric a little distance from where it emerged, holding the "tail" of the thread taut and flat to the fabric.

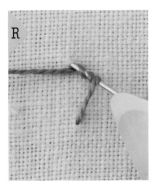 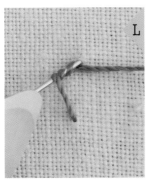

3. Take the needle and thread through to the back of the fabric. Hold the knot with your thumb as you pull the thread through to the back of the fabric.

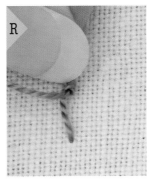 

◊ Pistil stitch

◊ Work as many stitches as your design requires.

◊ Pistil stitch worked in perle cotton #8

Running Stitch

Running stitch is also known as darning stitch, as many darning patterns are created using it.

1. Simply pass the needle over and under the fabric in a regular, even manner.

◇ Running stitch

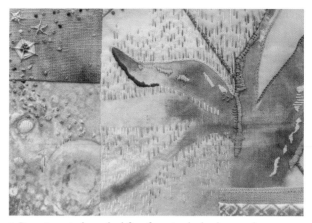

◇ Running stitch worked free-form in the background

Pattern darning creates very attractive designs by changing the length of the stitches and the spacing between them.

◇ Pattern darning can look effective if you use a variegated thread.

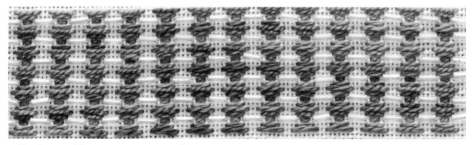

◇ Beads spaced between running stitches

Running Stitch (Stepped and Threaded 1)

Stepped and threaded running stitch 1 creates a line which can take on a braidlike appearance. It can be used just as it is, or further decorated with stitches or beads. To create more interest, you can also use novelty threads at the lacing stage.

1. Work 2 parallel rows of running stitch (previous page). "Step," or offset the stitches in the second row

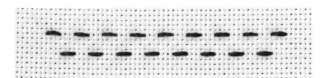

2. Thread a blunt-ended tapestry needle with a second thread. This needle will help you avoid splitting the foundation running stitches. Bring the thread out on the bottom line and pass the needle diagonally under the first bottom and top stitches.

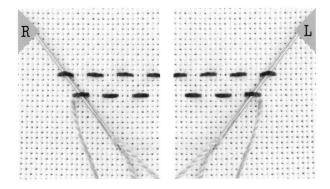

3. Pull the thread through. Turn the needle and slide it under the second top running stitch and the first bottom running stitch.

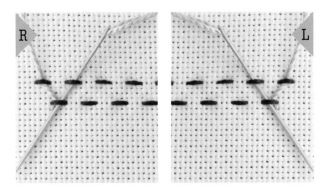

4. Pull the thread through and repeat along the line. As you move from stitch to stitch, do not pass the needle through the ground fabric.

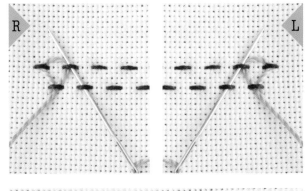

◇ A line of stepped and threaded running stitch 1

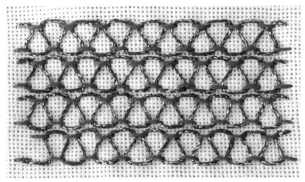

⁑ Stepped and threaded running stitch worked row upon row and threaded with a metallic yarn

◊ Stepped and threaded running stitch decorating a seam in crazy quilting

Running Stitch (Stepped and Threaded 2)

Stepped and threaded running stitch 2 creates a line which can look like a braid, if worked closely spaced together. As you move from row to row, do not pass the needle through the ground fabric.

1. Work 2 parallel foundation rows of running stitches (page 156), offsetting the second row.

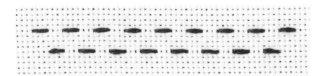

2. Thread a blunt-ended tapestry needle with a second thread. This needle will help you avoid splitting the foundation running stitches. Bring the thread out on the top line and pass the needle diagonally under the first top and bottom stitches.

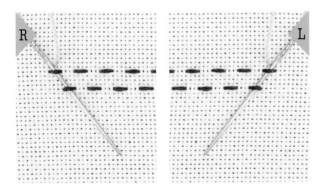

3. Turn the needle and pass it first under the lacing thread, then under the next running stitch on the top row. Pull the thread through.

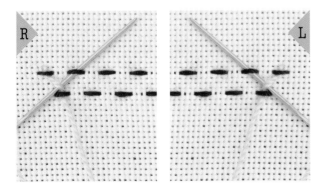

4. Turn your needle and slide it under the lacing thread, then under the next running stitch on the bottom row. Pull your thread through.

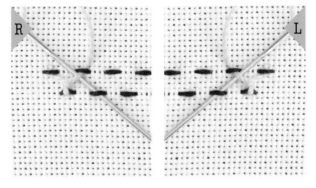

5. Continue these lacing steps along the line.

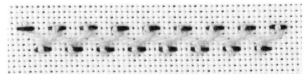

◇ A line of stepped and threaded running stitch 2

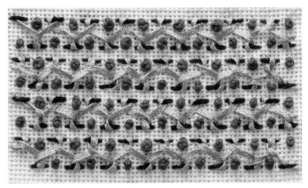

⸙ Stepped and threaded running stitch 2 laced with a fine ribbon

Running Stitch (Threaded)

Threaded running stitch makes an attractive threaded line, which follows curves well.

1. Work a line of running stitch (page 156).

2. Using a blunt-tipped tapestry needle, thread the stitches with a contrasting color or weight of thread. Take care to lace under the stitches only, *not* under the fabric.

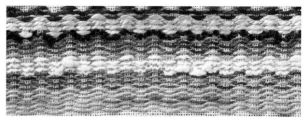

This stitch becomes interesting when you lace with a different thread. Here, I have used silk, novelty yarn, and perle cotton #5 and #8.

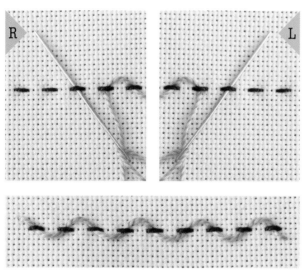

Another approach is to work 2 or 3 lines of running stitch as a foundation row. Here, the rows are worked face to face and bugle beads are added to the spaces created in the pattern.

◊ A line of threaded running stitch

A foundation row of 2 lines of running stitch was worked in perle cotton #5 before lacing in both directions with a metallic thread.

◊ The upper right corner above the crab is threaded running stitch worked in a variety of threads.

Satin Stitch

Satin stitch is one of the oldest embroidery stitches and is found on traditional embroideries in practically every country of the globe. To use satin stitch to advantage, stitches should lie evenly and closely together.

Tension can be an issue for some people. If your stitches are too slack or too tight, use an embroidery hoop.

This stitch is really suitable for covering small areas only, as long satin stitches can snag and become loose and untidy. If holding a neat, curved edge is difficult, try using outlined satin stitch (page 163) to solve the problem. If you need to cover a larger area, divide the shape into smaller sections and work rows of satin stitch to fill each area.

1. Make a single straight stitch.

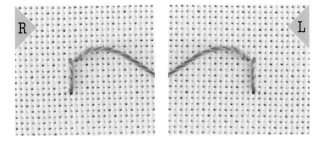

2. Bring the needle out very close to the stitch just made and continue to work the line or fill the shape.

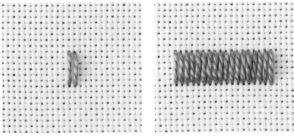

◇ Satin stitch worked in a line

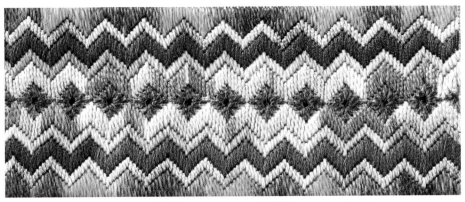

◇ Satin stitch worked in variegated perle cotton #5. I worked them in a simple zigzag pattern.

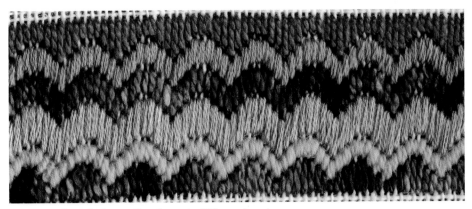

◇ Satin stitch worked in scallop shapes in different threads

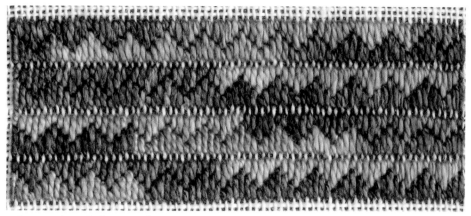

◇ Satin stitch worked in a regular patterns using a variegated perle cotton #5

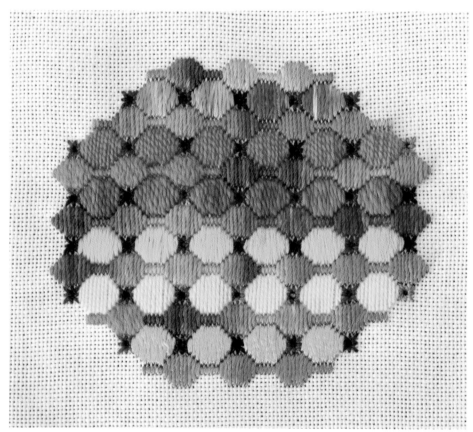

⧓ Different threads were used in this sample of satin stitch and Algerian eye stitch (page 28). Silk,
⧓ linen, and perle cotton #5 are used.

⧓ You do not have to cover the whole surface of the fabric. Here, rows of satin stitch are spaced
⧓ apart. The pattern was worked using variegated perle cotton #5.

Satin Stitch (Outlined)

Outlined satin stitch is ideal for adding an even edge to a shape. It is created by working straight stitches close together over an outline of chain stitches (page 80). It produces a neat, uniformly edged, filling stitch.

Tip If your stitches are too slack so that they sag, or too tight so that they pucker the fabric, use an embroidery hoop.

1. Mark your shape on fabric using an erasable or dissolving pen. Work the outline in chain stitch (page 80).

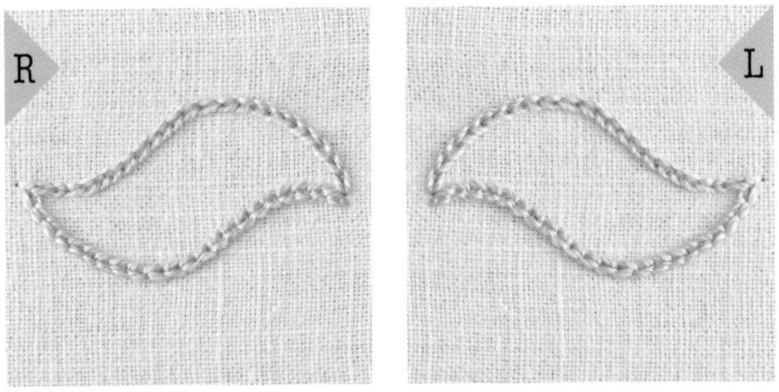

2. Starting at one edge, bring the thread up close to the line and work straight stitches very close together, but not on top of each other.

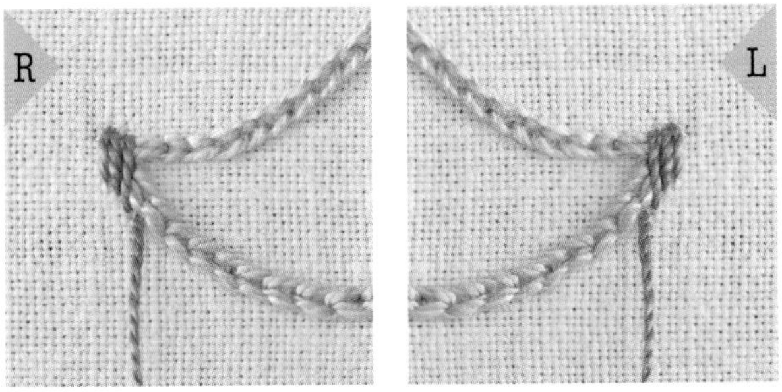

3. Continue working straight stitches side by side until you fill the shape.

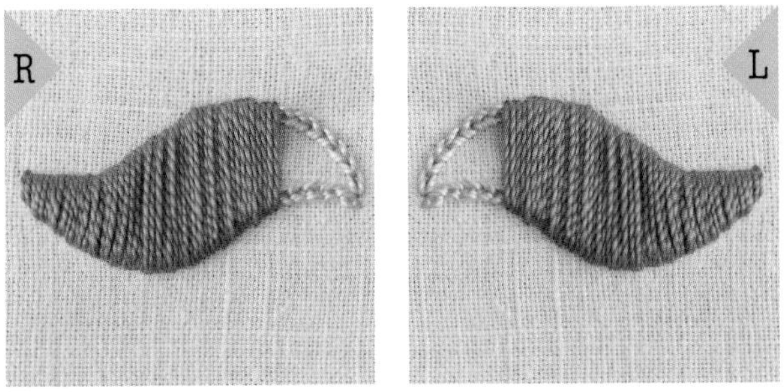

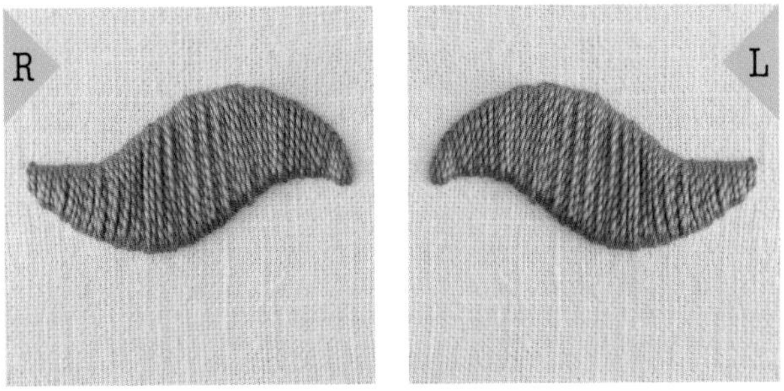

◇ A filled shape using outlined satin stitch

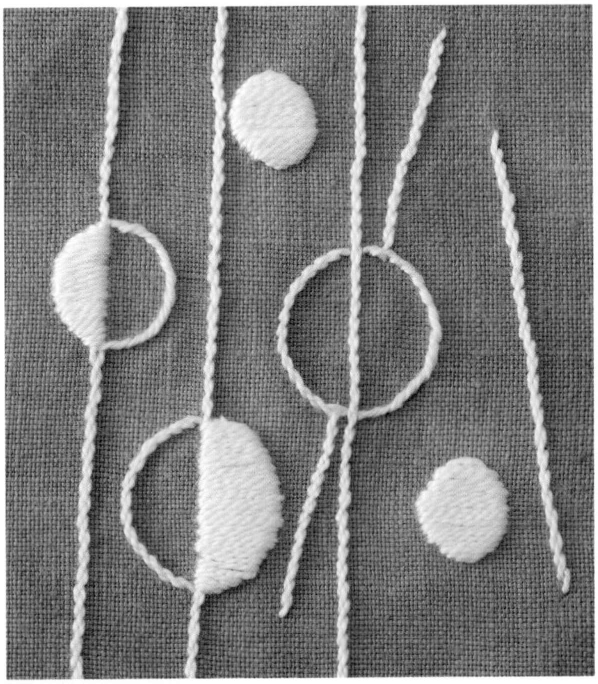

Outlined satin stitch used to define small circles. The sample is worked in perle cotton #8 on hand-dyed linen.

Satin Stitch (Padded)

Padded satin stitch is a very effective way to define and emphasize an area in your embroidery.

1. Work 3–5 long straight stitches using a thicker thread or 6 strands of cotton floss.

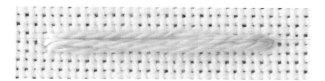

2. Make a straight stitch across the foundation stitches at one end. Make another straight stitch very close to the first. Make sure you take the needle to the back of the fabric, so you are stitching through the fabric, not just wrapping the padding stitches.

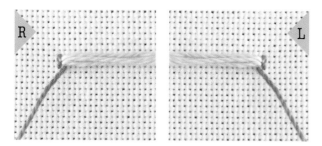

3. Continue to cover the padding evenly. When completed, only the satin stitches should show.

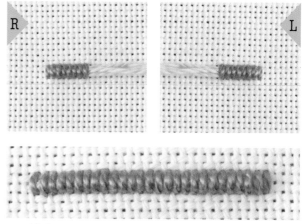

◊ Padded satin stitch in a row

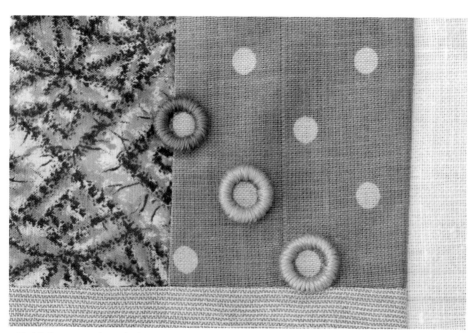

◊ Padded satin stitch worked in rings

Scroll Stitch

Scroll stitch will hold a tight curve and can be worked back to back to produce a heavy braidlike line. This stitch looks good in thicker threads and novelty threads, so do experiment a bit.

1. Work scroll stitch from left to right along a line. Bring your needle out on the left and take a small bite of the fabric on the line. With the thread wrapped behind and under the needle, pull it through the fabric.

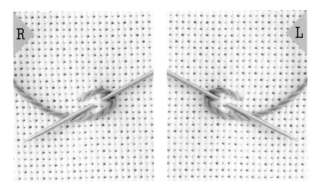

2. Do not pull the loop too tightly.

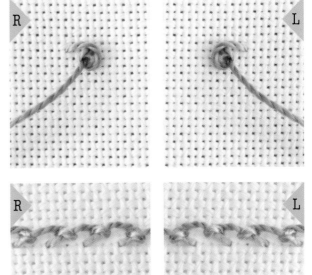

A line of scroll stitch. This sample was worked in perle cotton #5. However, I encourage you to experiment with threads, as this stitch looks good worked in thicker threads.

◇ Scroll stitch worked a series of scallops along a seam on a crazy quilt block

Sheaf Stitch

Sheaf stitch is a quick, easily worked stitch that looks good in a firmly twisted thread such as perle cotton #5 or #8.

1. Bring the needle out at the top of where you want your stitch to be and make a vertical straight stitch. This stitch will be the middle stitch of the sheaf.

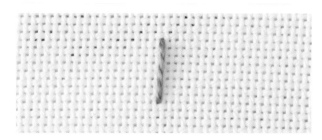

2. Make a second straight stitch to the right (left) of the first. Make a third vertical stitch bringing the needle out to the left (right) of the center stitch as illustrated. Pull the thread through.

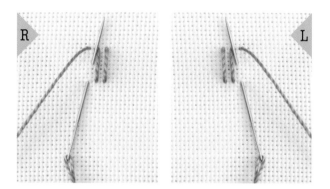

3. Thread the needle under the left (right) straight stitch.

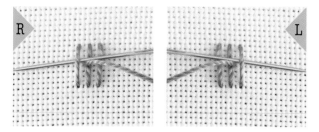

4. Take the thread over the top and pass the needle under the right (left) straight stitch. Insert the needle in the middle and take the thread to the back.

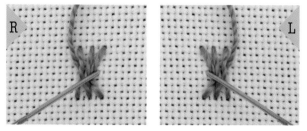

5. Pull it snug to make a small cross bar and give the sheaf a waist.

◊ Completed sheaf stitch

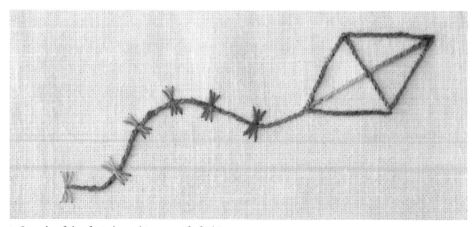

◊ Sample of sheaf stitch used in a motif of a kite

Stem Stitch

This linear stitch is incredibly useful because it can hold a curve well and looks good in variety of threads.

1. Work from left to right (right to left for left-handed). Bring the thread up from the back of the fabric on the line.

With your working thread under your needle, make a small backward stitch.

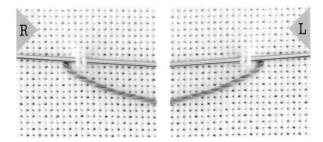

2. Pull the thread through the fabric.

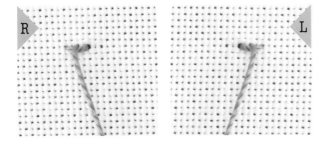

3. Make the second stitch forward along the line, bringing the needle out a little behind the first stitch. Pull the thread through the fabric.

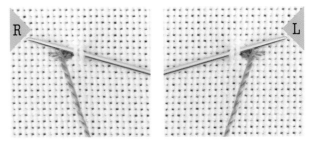

4. Repeat along the line. Keep stitches the same length and the tension even. Closely spaced stitches make a tight line. You can make a looser line by lengthening the spacing.

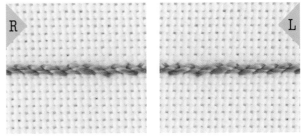

◇ A line of stem stitch

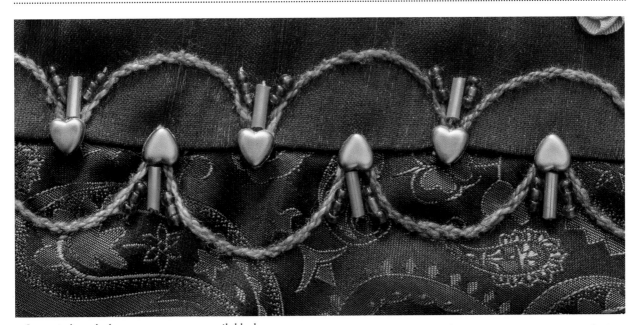

◇ Stem stitch worked on a seam on a crazy quilt block.

◇ Stem stitch worked along the edge of a piece of silk appliquéd with Mistyfuse (by Attached Inc.)

Stem Stitch (Portuguese)

Portuguese stem stitch creates a knotted, ropelike line which can be accentuated by using a heavy solid twisted thread, such as pearl cotton.

Portuguese stem is best used when you want a chunkier, stronger stitch. It can be used on even-weave or plain fabrics and follows a curve well.

1. Portuguese stem is best worked starting at the bottom and working toward the top. Bring the thread through from the back of the fabric and pick up a small piece of material.

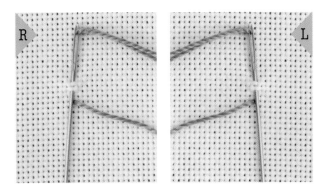

2. Bring the thread out to left (right). Slide the needle under the first stitch. Make sure you do not pick up any fabric.

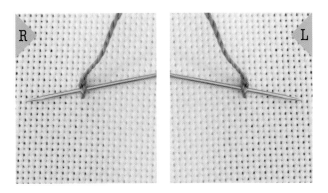

3. Take the needle through. You are actually whipping this stitch.

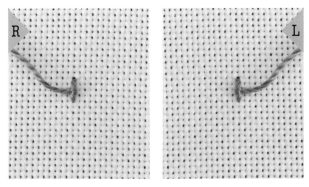

4. Whip the stitch a second time under the first whipped stitch. These 2 whipping stitches form the knotlike appearance.

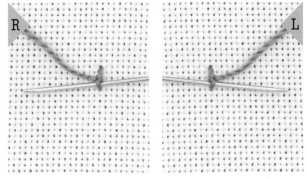

5. Move along the line and make another small stitch.

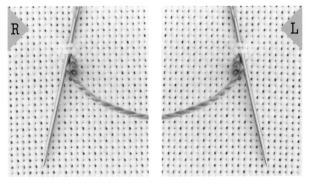

6. Repeat the whipping process on the first and second stitch. Continue up the line.

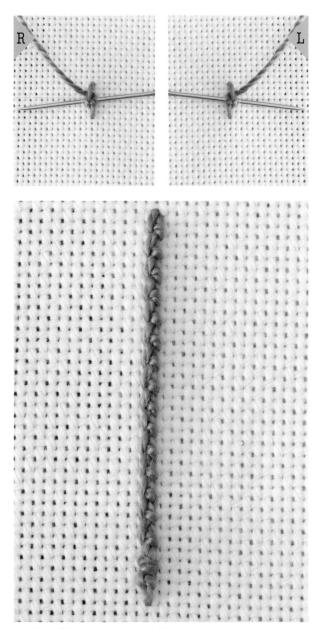

◇ A line of Portuguese stem stitch

◇ Portuguese stem stitch used on a crazy quilt block

Stem Stitch (Whipped)

Whipped stem stitch creates a slightly raised line that can look like a fine cord.

For the whipping thread, you have the option of switching the color, thread thickness, or thread texture.

1. Work a foundation row of stem stitches (page 167). Make each stitch slightly longer and looser than usual, so you can pass a second thread under them more easily.

2. Use a blunt tapestry needle for the second thread, so that you do not split the foundation threads as you sew. Bring the needle from the back of the fabric and pass it under the first 2 stitches. Do not pick up any of the fabric.

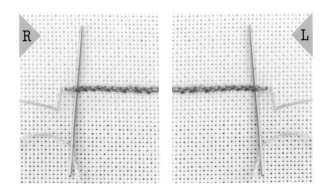

3. Take the thread over the top of the stitches and pass the needle under the second and third stem stitches. Do not pick up any of the fabric.

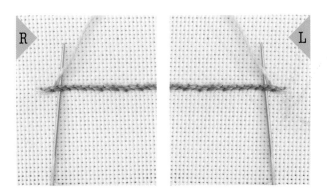

4. Repeat along the entire length of the row.

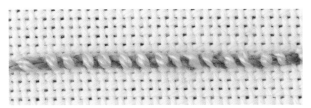

◇ Completed row of whipped stem stitch

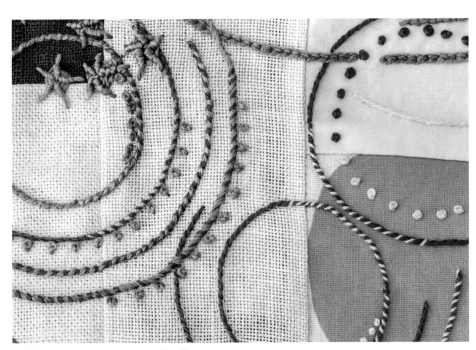

◇ Whipped stem stitch on a small wall piece

Turkman Stitch

Some embroiderers classify Turkman stitch as a form of chain stitch (page 80), and others classify it as a closed feather stitch (page 124). This stitch could be either. No matter which it is, Turkman stitch is simple and quick and will follow a gentle curve. You can easily decorate it further by using the spaces created by the stitch.

1. Work between 2 imaginary vertical lines. Bring the needle out at the top left (right), insert it on the top right (left), and make a small vertical stitch so that the needle point reappears on the right (left) line. Keeping the thread under the needle point, pull the thread through.

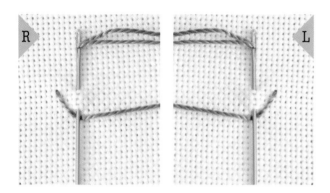

2. Insert the needle on the left (right) line, very close to where the thread emerged, and take a small vertical bite. Keeping the thread under the needle point, pull the thread through.

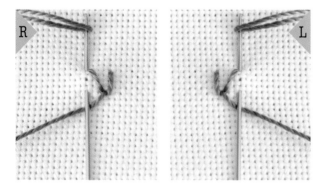

3. Insert the needle on the right (left) line, catching the loop, and make a small vertical stitch.

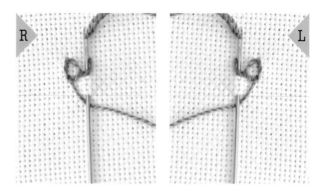

4. Alternate down the row, making sure that each stitch catches the previous stitch.

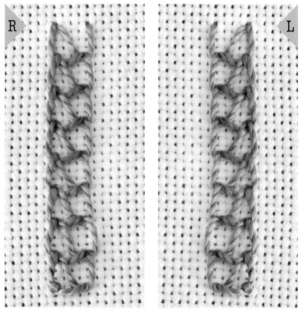

◇ Completed line of Turkman stitch

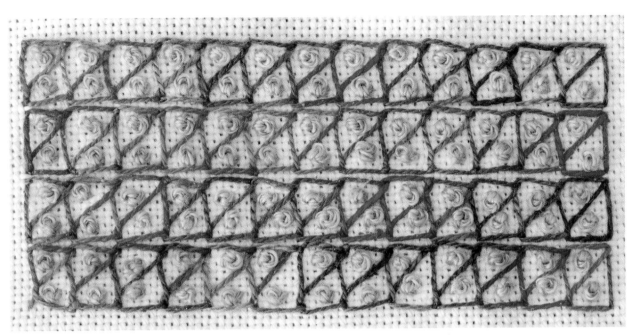

◇ Turkman stitch worked in perle cotton #5 and further decorated with French knots (page 135)

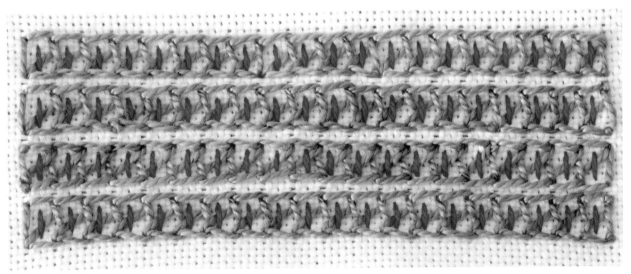

◇ Turkman stitch worked in perle cotton #5 and tied with a cross bar

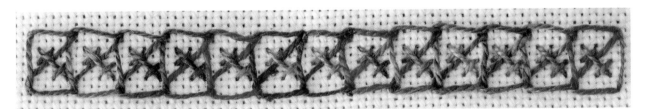

◇ There are many opportunities to fill the spaces in this stitch with extra decoration.

Van Dyke Stitch

Van Dyke stitch is traditionally used as a border. By varying the width, you can create nice leaf shapes that have a central line up the spine of the design. Van Dyke stitch looks good worked in thread with a firm twist such as a perle cotton #5 or #8.

Tip Keep your tension slightly loose. If you pull the stitches too tightly, the center plaited line will not form nicely.

1. This stitch is worked between 2 invisible vertical lines. If needed, you can mark the outline with a disappearing marker pen. Bring the thread out on the left. Move up diagonally and make a small horizontal stitch at the center point of the stitch.

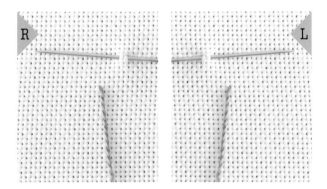

2. Pull the needle through and insert it on the right (left) (right) line. The working thread should make a narrow cross. Bring the needle out on the left (right) line, a little below the first stitch.

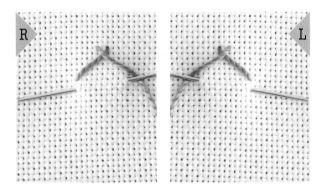

3. Pass the needle behind the 2 long diagonal stitches, taking care not to pick up any fabric.

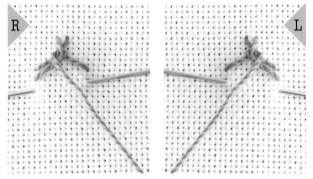

4. Take the needle to the back of the fabric on the right (left) side of the line and bring it out on the left (right), just below the stitch.

5. Continue working down the line.

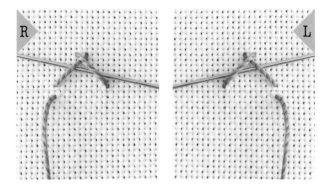

◇ Completed Van Dyke stitch

Wheat Ear Stitch

Wheat ear stitch is an easy, versatile stitch that is often used to depict wild grasses and wheat. This stitch will follow a curve well or can be worked in single units and arranged in patterns. The length of the diagonal stitches can be varied, and it lends itself to beading. Many types of embroidery thread can be used. It is a stitch that can easily be laced or threaded, and you can use the rows to couch down the thread.

1. Make a straight stitch worked at an angle.

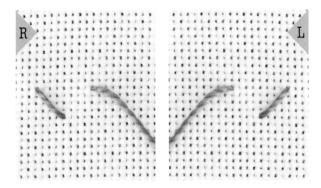

2. Make a second straight stitch in the opposite angle, with the base touching the base of the first stitch. Bring your thread out a little below the base of the V.

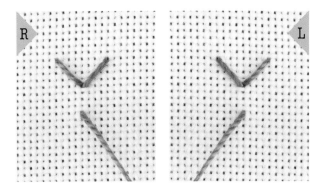

3. Pass the needle under the 2 straight stitches.

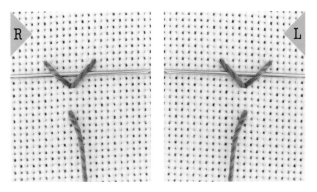

4. Pull the needle through and take it to the back of the fabric so that the thread loops in a single chain

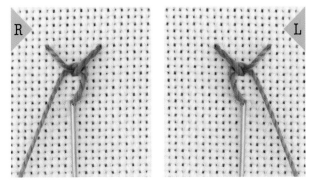

5. At this stage, this unit is a single detached wheat ear stitch and you can arrange these units in patterns.

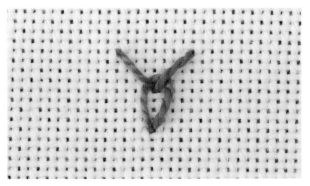

6. To make a row, add another set of diagonal stitches and bring the thread out further down the line.

7. Pass the needle under the 2 stitches to make the chainlike loop and continue down the line.

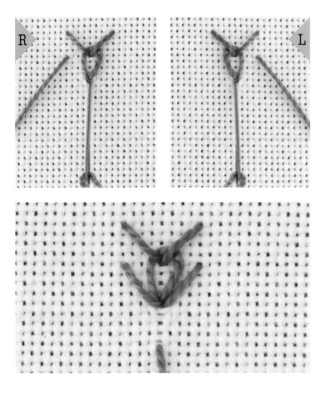

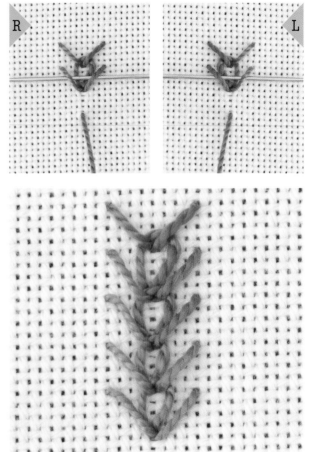

◊ A line of wheat ear stitch

◊ The grasses were created using a variety of wheat ear stitches.

Wheat Ear Stitch (Alternating)

Alternating wheat ear stitch can be used to create unusual border patterns. This stitch will follow a curve well or can be worked in single units.

1. Start with a straight stitch worked at an angle.

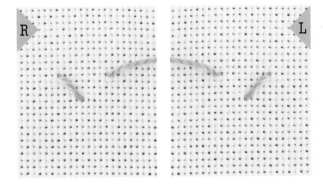

2. Make 3 straight stitches at an angle in the opposite direction. Make sure the base of each stitch is in the same hole as the first stitch. Bring the thread out a little below the base.

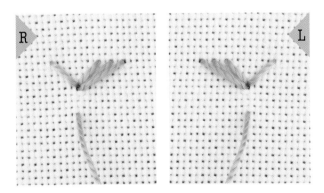

3. Pass the needle under the straight stitches.

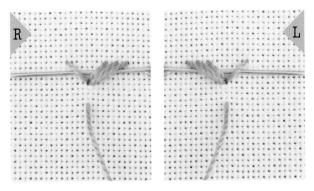

4. Take the needle through the fabric so that the thread loops in a single chain.

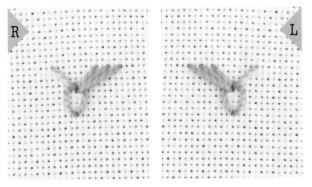

5. Work 3 straight stitches on the other side of the line, into the base of the chain stitch.

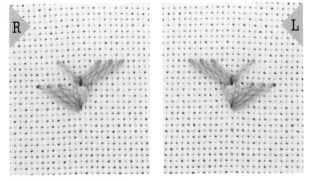

6. Add a single stitch to the other side and bring your thread out further down the line.

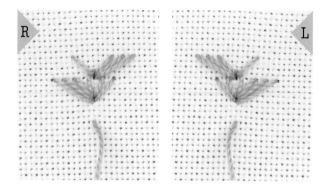

◇ Alternating wheat ear stitch

7. Pass the needle under the 4 stitches to make another chainlike loop and continue in this manner down the line.

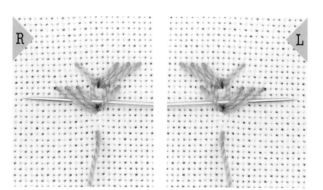

◇ Alternating wheat ear stitch in variegated perle cotton #5

Wheat Ear Stitch (Chevron)

Chevron wheat ear stitch can be used to create unusual border patterns. If you work just a single line of this stitch, it will follow a curve well. It is very similar to regular wheat ear (page 175), but with extra straight stitches added to the V section of the stitch. Changing the angle of the straight stitches and changing the spacing between the lines can vary the pattern.

1. Start with 4 straight stitches worked at an angle. Bring the needle out a little below the base.

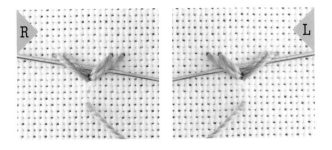

2. Pass the needle under the straight stitches.

3. Pull the needle under the stitches and take it through the fabric so that the thread loops in a single chain.

4. Work another set of 4 straight stitches into the base of the chain stitch. Bring your thread out further down the line.

5. Continue until you have a line of stitches.

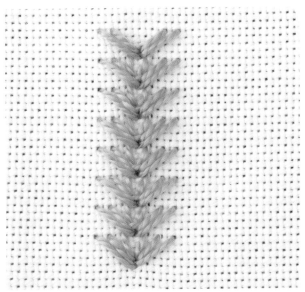

6. Turn your work and commence the next line of stitches.

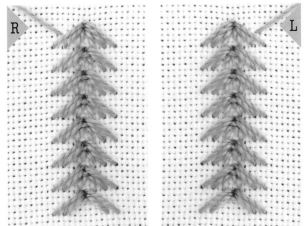

7. Work a set of 4 straight stitches.

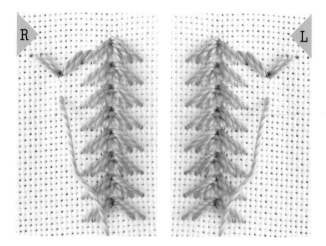

8. Continue the pattern down the line.

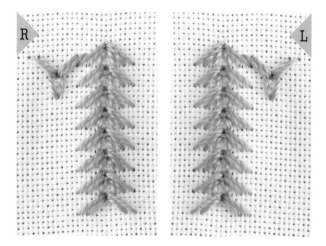

9. Work each line in the opposite direction, turning your work at the end of each line. Work as many lines of chevron wheat ear stitch as you need to fill the area of your design.

◊ Chevron wheat ear stitch

Whipped Spoke Stitch

Whipped spoke stitch produces a line of ridged stitches. It can be used alone as an accent stitch, or to produce a textured filling. It can be very dramatic, as it forms a strong line. Use variegated threads, novelty threads, or even fine knitting yarns to whip the spokes.

1. Lay down foundation stitches of straight stitch, in the shape you wish to work.

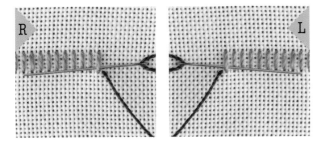

2. Use a blunt tapestry needle to avoid splitting the foundation stitches. Bring the thread up at the bottom of the line and slide the needle under 1 thread and pull it through. Move back to the start and slide the needle under 2 threads. Note that the needle does not go through the fabric.

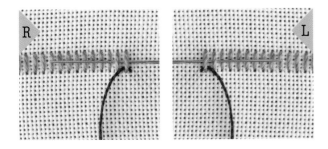

3. Pull the thread through, and you have whipped the first spoke.

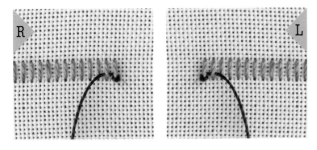

4. For the rest of the line, slide the needle under 2 threads, pull it through, move back 1 thread, and slide the needle under 2 threads.

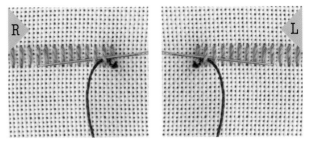

5. Repeat this action, whipping each spoke as you progress along the line.

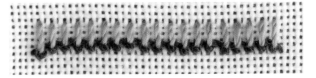

6. When you have finished the first row, take the needle through the fabric to where you began and work a second row, then a third and so on until the rows fill the shape.

◇ A line of whipped spoke stitch

§ Whipped spoke stitch is worked in a fan shape in combination
§ with French knots (page 135) on a crazy quilt seam.

◇ Whipped spoke stitch used around a bead

◇ Fans of whipped spoke stitch used to secure a bead

Whipped Wheel

Whipped wheel creates a ribbed disk that can be used as single accent stitch.

1. Start with a single fly stitch (page 131). To each side of the fly stitch tail, add 2 straight stitches of equal length. You should have a circle which has five "spokes" to form the foundation.

2. Bring your thread up at the center of the wheel.

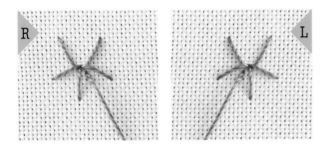

3. From this point on, your needle does not go through the fabric, so use a blunt tapestry needle to avoid splitting the foundation stitches. Slide the needle under 2 threads and pull the thread through.

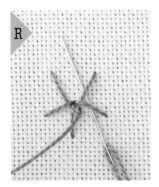

4. Move back 1 stitch and slide the needle under 2 threads. Pull the thread through and you have whipped the first spoke. This process is best described as making a spiral of backstitches over the spokes

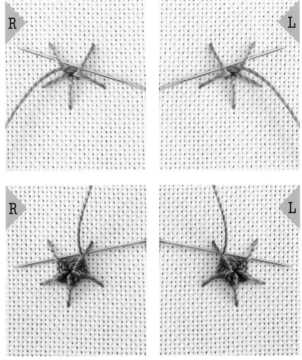

5. Repeat this action, whipping each spoke as you progress around the wheel until the circle is filled.

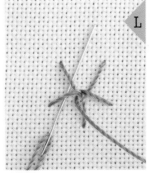

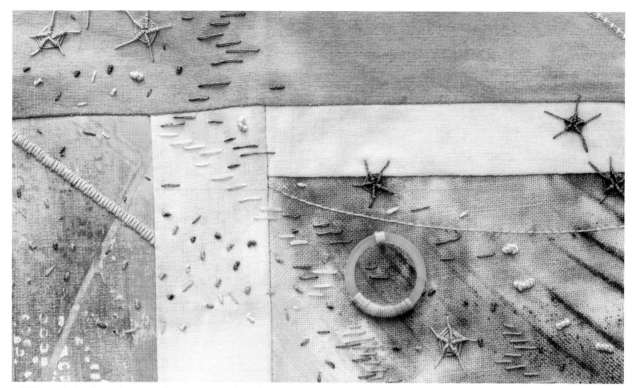

◇ Whipped wheels worked in perle cotton #8 and used as accent stitches

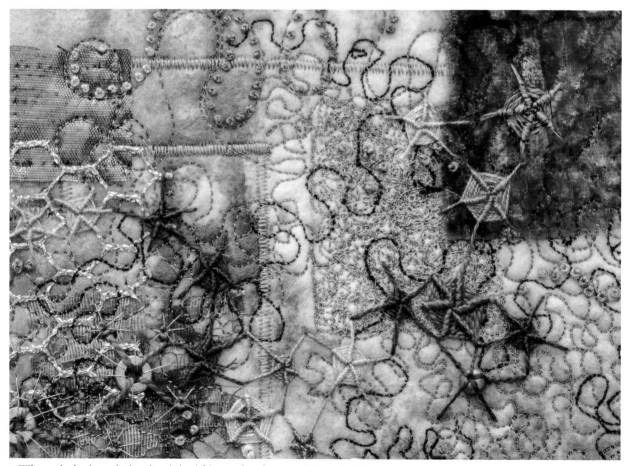

◇ Whipped wheels worked on hand-dyed felt over free-form machine embroidery

Whipped Wheel (Over-a-Bead)

1. Secure the bead to the fabric with 5 straight stitches that will form the foundation of the stitch.

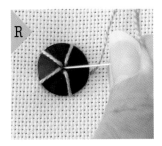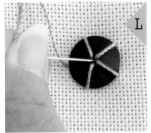

2. Bring the thread up at the center of the bead. From this point onward, your needle does not go through the fabric. Slide the needle under 2 threads and pull it through.

3. Move back 1 stitch and slide the needle under 2 threads. Pull the thread through and you have whipped the first spoke.

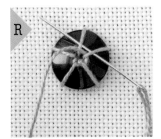

4. Continue around, whipping each spoke as you progress around the wheel, until the circle is as large as you want it to be. To finish, slide the needle under the whipped area and take it down through the center of the bead.

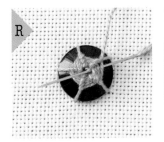

◊ Whipped wheel over-a-bead

⸙ Whipped wheel over irregular coconut beads, alongside
⸙ French knots (page 135) and buttonhole wheels (page 68)

Woven Trellis Stitch

To make woven trellis, you work a group of foundation stitches onto which you weave. Use a blunt tapestry needle so that, as you weave the threads, you do not split them by accident.

1. Start by working 12 straight stitches clustered in groups of 3, arranged radiating from the middle.

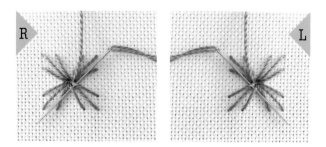

2. Bring the working thread up through the fabric at the middle. Begin weaving by sliding the needle under the 2 outer threads, skipping the middle thread. Pull the thread through firmly, but not too tight.

3. Turn the needle and continue weaving by picking the middle thread of the same group. Pull the thread through and continue in this back-and-forth motion.

4. As you weave, use the needle to pack the petal so that it firm.

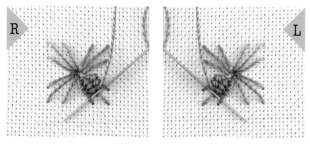

5. Continue weaving until it is packed firmly to the base. Take the thread to the back and bring it out at the center of the motif ready to work the next set of foundation stitches.

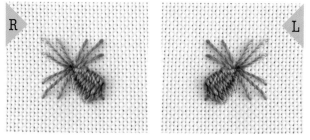

6. Work until each section is woven and take the thread to the back and secure it with 2 small backstitches.

◇ Woven trellis

❃ You can vary this stitch by working it in parts. This sample illustrates a quarter of woven trellis worked between the scallops on a crazy quilt seam.

Woven Trellis Stitch (Over-a-Bead)

Woven trellis over-a-bead is worked in the same way as regular woven trellis (previous page), but you use the 12 straight stitches to secure the bead. If you want to add texture to your work, use a low, flat bead. If you want to use a higher bead, the bead will show, becoming a novel way to attach a bead.

1. Start by using 12 straight stitches to secure the bead. Arrange them in groups of 3 radiating from the middle.

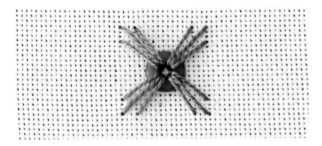

2. Bring the working thread up through the bead at the middle. See woven trellis stitch (previous page) to weave the base stitches.

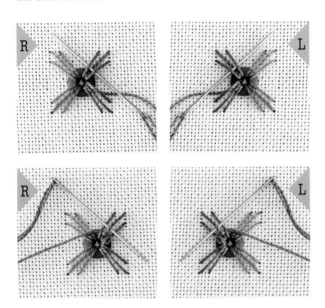

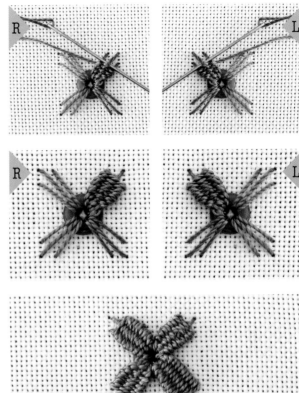

◇ Woven trellis over-a-bead

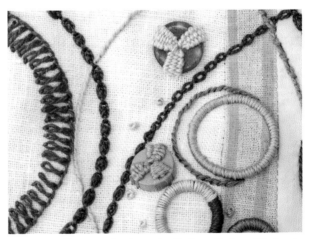

Woven trellis over-a-bead in a detail of a wall piece. The beads are large and I wove only 9 straight stitches so the beads could be seen.

Index